Advanced Placement Study Guide

Greg Sherwin

Paul T. Gray, Jr.

Parisa Meymand

Human Geography

People, Place, and Culture

Eleventh Edition

Sanya Bawa

WILEY

For our children and grandchildren

Carter Sherwin, Dylan Sherwin, Zach Gray, Ariston Gray, Jenny Gray, Grayden McElroy, Emma McElroy, Sophie Watson, Lily Watson

Go out and explore the world of opportunities

Front-cover photo: Alexander B. Murphy

Founded in 1807, John Wiley & Sons, Inc., has been a valued source of knowledge and understanding for more than 200 years, helping people around the world meet their needs and fulfill their aspirations. Our company is built on a foundation of principles that include responsibility to the communities we serve and where we live and work. In 2008, we launched a Corporate Citizenship Initiative, a global effort to address the environmental, social, economic, and ethical challenges we face in our business. Among the issues we are addressing are carbon impact, paper specifications and procurement, ethical conduct within our business and among our vendors, and community and charitable support. For more information, please visit our website: *www.wiley.com/go/citizenship*.

ISBN 978-1-119-11934-0

Printed in the United States of America

10 9 8 7 6 5 4

Printed and bound by Bind-Rite/Robbinsville

The Most Important Page in the Book
(Formerly known as the Preface)

Why is this the MOST IMPORTANT PAGE IN THE BOOK? Well, the simple answer to that question is that this is where we explain how the book is laid out. Certainly, once you look at the table of contents you probably will get a generally idea, but we really want you to understand the purpose of the book.

So, here it is … our goal is to help you be successful in your AP Human Geography class. And we really want this book to be user friendly and very flexible.

We have three simple major goals in this book, and therefore, we organized the book into three parts.

1. **Understanding AP Human Geography and your textbook:** Our goal is to introduce you to the course. We explain what AP Human Geography is, how the class is organized, and how your textbook is organized. We end by explaining how the chapter-by-chapter study tool works.

2. **Understanding your textbook:** Our goal is to provide a chapter-by-chapter study tool in order to help you better comprehend what you have read. We call it our "Five Steps to Chapter Success," and we know your understanding of your textbook will improve following the five-step plan.

3. **Understanding the AP Exam:** The final section is designed to help you prepare for the AP exam. We will give you study tools and a practice exam in order to better prepare you for the test.

In essence, this study guide is like three books in one, or if you like:

This book is like an amazing ice cream sandwich, with Part 2 being the incredible ice cream filling between two delicious chocolate cookies. (Please try to refrain from biting the book—it is just a yummy metaphor.)

And let's just say for a second that you don't like chocolate and you only want ice cream! Well, you can just jump right into Part 2 of the book and sink your teeth into the middle. (Don't read too quickly or you might get an ice cream headache.)

Or if you just want one cookie, you can jump to Part 3 and prepare for the AP exam.

We believe that the beauty of the book is that it can stay with you throughout the entire year or be used when you want. The only thing better is if it came in a scratch and sniff version.

Teacher's note: The authors of this book, *Human Geography: Advanced Placement Study Guide* are teachers with over 40 years of combined experience teaching the class. Through their years of teaching, they have included many ideas on how to structure the class. And they have tried to capture the high school mindset and to structure the book in a way that a teenager would appreciate, injecting humor at times and giving clues to important aspects of the class in simple ways.

TABLE OF CONTENTS

PART 1: Understanding AP Human Geography **1**

Section 1: Why Everyone Needs to Take Human Geography: 1
It's a Smaller World after All

Section 2: This Ain't Yo Daddy's or Momma's Geography 7

Section 3: How to Read Your Textbook or 18
How This Workbook Saved My Grade

PART 2: Understanding Your Textbook **29**

Chapter 1: Introduction to Human Geography 29
Chapter 2: Population 38
Chapter 3: Migration 49
Chapter 4: Local Culture, Popular Culture, and Cultural Landscapes 59
Chapter 5: Identity: Race, Ethnicity, Gender, and Sexuality 67
Chapter 6: Language 75
Chapter 7: Religion 85
Chapter 8: Political Geography 95
Chapter 9: Urban Geography 104
Chapter 10: Development 113
Chapter 11: Agriculture and the Rural Landscape 122
Chapter 12: Industry and Services 132
Chapter 13: The Humanized Environment 141
Chapter 14: Globalization and the Geography of Networks 151

Part 3: Getting Ready for the AP Exam **158**

Section 1: Anatomy of a Multiple-Choice Question 159

Section 2: Anatomy of a Free-Response Question 166

Section 3: Practice Exam #1 169

Section 4: Practice Exam #2 190

Part 1 Section 1: Why everyone needs to take Human Geography: It's a smaller world after all

Courtesy Gregory Sherwin

Purpose

Buckle up and get excited about taking the most important class in your life! Have your passports ready because you will travel the world in AP Human Geography. There are only a few classes that you will take in your lifetime that will give you information that will stay with you the rest of your years.

Human Geography is one of those courses!

We've divided this section into four parts:

A. Introduction: You Need This Class!

B. Why Americans Are Geographically Challenged (Part 1)

C. Why Americans Are Geographically Challenged (Part 2)

D. Conclusion: You Need This Class!

Reykjavik, Iceland. Author Gregory Sherwin in front of a traditional sod house in Iceland. Sod houses insulated people from harsh winds and cold winters.

A. Introduction: You Need This Class!

We live in an era of globalization and interdependence, with countries and people interacting with each other at a more regular and rapid rate. As the Disney song goes, "It's a small world after all," and with technology becoming an integral part of everyday life, the world continues to shrink. So, in fact, it is a smaller and smaller world after all (there is actually a concept we will learn later called *time–space compression* that geographers use to illustrate this idea).

Dr. Michael P. Peterson at the Department of Geography/Geology, University of Nebraska at Omaha, summarizes the idea of globalization and the importance of geography in today's world

> In a world so shrunken in distance and time that you can almost instantly communicate with any other city on any other continent, and in which you can fly to virtually its remotest corner in a matter of hours, a knowledge of differing peoples and places can no longer be considered the luxury of a few, but is, instead, a necessity of every individual.
>
> Our interdependence is so complete that business decisions taken in Tokyo and Singapore have repercussions in Copenhagen and Peoria. Just to stay abreast of world events requires that we learn not only where these events are occurring, but also why they are taking place and how they will impact on our lives. **Such considerations are the very essence of geography.**

Wow! What a powerful quote. Now, ask yourself these questions:

1. **What more important course is there for you to take in a post–September 11 world?**
2. **What is going to get you better prepared to compete in a global marketplace?**
3. **What is going to better prepare you to deal with the diversity of the workplace in America today?**

Reread the quote again—stop and chew on each part. After you think about these questions and pose your own, you should come to the conclusion that geography most effectively teaches these concepts. It is a smaller world after all, and geography is one of the few courses specifically designed to prepare you for this world.

> Thinking geographically is important. You need to know about the world because the world is deeply connected. Those who lack global understanding will be left behind.

B. Why Americans Are Geographically Challenged (Part 1)

Americans are geographically challenged. We don't know much about geography, and geography was never a pressing issue in American education. Why is that? Well, the irony is that the actual geography of North America has allowed the people who live there to not learn geography—in other words, to be geographically ignorant.

> The United States and Canada have historically been isolated by political borders and physical geography.

Think about the twentieth century for a second. Because of the luxury of its location in the Western Hemisphere, the United States was late in getting involved in two world wars. Why?

Because we were separated from the conflict—our geography isolated us. Separated by two oceans and with no country in turmoil on our borders, we could afford to watch troubles unfold and think about whether or not to get involved and when.

And yes, Pearl Harbor did bring the United States into World War II, but think about that attack for a moment. At that time, Hawaii was a territory. Nestled in the Pacific Ocean, Hawaii was the best geographic target for Japan to attack, but Hawaii was far removed from the continental United States. Think again for a second. Although the Japanese were able to attack Pearl Harbor, where else in the United States did they attack? And why didn't Japan take control of Hawaii after the attack? Again the answer lies in American geography.

According to Russell Bova, in a book titled *How the World Works:*

> No war has been fought on American soil since the Civil War, and the last time foreign troops fought on American territory was the War of 1812. Americans have experienced terrorist attacks on the homeland, such as the September 11, 2001, attacks on the World Trade Center and the Pentagon, but no American alive today has ever had foreign soldiers march across his or her property, has ever had to hide in a shelter while bombs rained from above, or has ever experienced the death of a child on U.S. soil at the hands of an enemy army.[1] So yes, we are telling you that Americans could afford to be geographically ignorant because our geography has protected us!

However, it is a smaller world after all, and the attacks on September 11 have proven that in a shrinking world with more interconnections, geographic isolation is no longer an option. Dr. Peterson's quote on page 2 illustrates the need for geography today.

> The World has become a more crowded, more interconnected, more volatile, and more unstable place. If education cannot help students see beyond themselves and better understand the interdependent nature of our world, then each new generation will remain ignorant, and its capacity to live competently and responsibly will be dangerously diminished.
>
> —Charles Fuller, geographer

It has been over a decade since September 11 and you would think Americans, especially young Americans 18 to 24 years of age, would know more about the world today. Well, think again …

C. Why Americans Are Geographically Challenged (Part 2)

In the past, there was a phrase to describe Americans' geographic ignorance. It went, "War is God's way of teaching Americans geography."[2] And whether it was Germany or Japan, Korea or Vietnam, we Americans, in the past, seemingly DID become interested in foreign countries and geography when we became involved in a conflict. We wanted to learn about where our soldiers were and who we were fighting. Yet, that was your parents' and your grandparents' generations. Today, we have gone from bad to worse. Today, we don't even bother to learn about the countries we're at war with!

According to a National Geographic study conducted in 2006[3]:

- ***Only 37 percent of young Americans could find Iraq on a map***—though U.S. forces had a major presence there from 2003 to 2011.

---

[1]How the World Works: A Brief Study of International Relations (New York: Longman, 2009), pp. 101–102.

[2] The Internet often attributes this quote to Ambrose Bierce, but according to the Ambrose Bierce website (donswaim.com), there is no record of him making this observation.

[3] http://www.nationalgeographic.com/roper2006/findings.html

- ***Almost 9 out of 10 young Americans (88 percent) could NOT find Afghanistan on a map of Asia***—this despite the presence of U.S. troops in the country since October 2001 and despite the fact that it is the longest conflict in American history.[4]
- ***Three-quarters (75 percent) of young Americans can NOT find Iran on a map***—this despite Iran being included in the Axis of Evil in 2002 by George W. Bush (the other two countries were Iraq and North Korea).
- ***Yep, you guessed it. Seven out of ten young Americans could NOT find North Korea on a map-*** What good is it having an Axis of Evil if you don't know where the evil is? But ask the directors of the movie *The Interview,* and you know that North Korea doesn't mess around.

"War. What is it good for?" So goes the lyrics to Edwin Starr's 1969 protest song. "Absolutely nothing" goes the response, and given that Americans can't find countries where we are fighting, it seems fairly accurate.

- ***Seven in ten (69 percent) young Americans can find China on a map!***

YES! It seems that China is one of the countries outside of North America that we can find (although 69 percent is still not the grade I want to see on my test). But hold on a minute: Young Americans still have a lot to learn about China, which is one of the most economically and politically dominant countries in the world. According to the survey, few (18 percent) Americans know that Mandarin Chinese is the most widely spoken native language in the world; 74 percent say it is English.

Do these results perhaps reflect a little ethnocentrism?

Ethnocentrism is a strong belief that your culture is the center of the universe. It was noted in the survey that Americans greatly overestimated the United States' population, thinking it was close to China's. Why? Because we're America and "We're #1!"—that's ethnocentrism. China's population is actually four times larger than that of the United States.

There was a time when U.S. students could be completely ethnocentric and isolated. Remember that our borders isolated us and that the United States was the foremost political, economic, and cultural power of the world. For decades, the United States would act and other countries would have to react. Basically, these relationships came down to the United States saying "jump" and other countries asking "how high?"

However, we believe that in the twenty-first century, the world has changed. The United States is a strong world power with huge dominance in the world, but its hegemony is in question as other countries are rising (China in particular).

Remember: The world is now a more crowded, more interconnected, more volatile, and more unstable place. In 2015, we are dealing with water and food shortages in some places of the world at the same time that some people are eating fresh food that was shipped around the globe. We are dealing with multinational corporations that have brought people from the world under one umbrella, and simultaneously we have religious warfare in Nigeria killing innocent people and dividing us further.

These issues of a more crowded, more interconnected, more volatile, an more unstable place exist in the United States also. The United States will become a majority minority country by

---

[4] This is, if you use the Gulf of Tonkin incident as the starting point for the Vietnam War (August 6, 1964). U.S. military involvement ended on August 15, 1973.

2030. That is, Caucasians will make up less than 50 percent of the population, and the United States will have more diversity. That diversity will surely lead to great possibilities, but also many potential problems. For example, issues of immigration from Latin America plague policy makers as to how to control the borders or what status we should give to "illegal immigrants".

These are all issues addressed in AP Human Geography and why we feel that AP Human Geography is the best suited class for students today. Do you need some more reasons? Keep on reading!

Side Note: Are you smarter than the average 18- to 24-year-old American? Go take the Geography test yourself (see http://www.nationalgeographic.com/roper2006).

D. Conclusion: You Need This Class!

We believe that this is the greatest class ever created. But we understand if you are a bit skeptical about this claim. So, don't take our words for it; here are some quotes from students who took the class.

> My favorite aspect of the course, and of geography as a whole, is the visual presentation of information on maps. The ability to learn so much about a subject in such a short amount of time is rarely equaled in any other subject matter. The class also looked at issues from both sides, giving a fair chance to every idea we were taught about. Because of my experiences in AP Human Geography I became interested in Urban and Economical geography and the two are connected. I am now pursuing a career in urban and regional planning. The class is practical for anyone looking to become more open minded and culturally sensitive. The class was the most influential and informative class I took while in high school.
>
> —Ben Lykins, 2010

> Human geography, contrary to my first impression, was much more than JUST geography. I learned about different ways of life, and it allowed me to see the world in a whole new way. Let's just say that from the beginning to the end of my sophomore year, it wasn't the world that changed, but my increased interest and awareness of 'the why of where' that changed my perspective. Now I can't even go to the mall without thinking about globalization!
>
> —Sammi Roth, 2011

> Human Geography is the study of the basis of human empirical nature. To understand human geography is to understand the collective actions of mankind.
>
> —Kevin Du, 2013

> Human Geography gave me one of the best experiences in high school I could have ever asked for. Human Geography made me more aware of the globalized world we live in! It's incredible to learn about different people throughout the world and the ways we are alike and different! I cannot drive by a McDonalds without thinking about globalization. Every time I see railroad tracks, I recognize that without these tracks, the suburbs I live in would not even exist. This class changed the way I look at life and I will be eternally grateful for that.
>
> —Sydney Goldberg, 2014

> Going into the course, I had a very narrow world view. I was unconcerned with other cultures and even more oblivious to the effect they had on my life. More than anything, human geography changed my future. I had always had a love for politics, but this course helped me discover that it's not the politics I love, but more the people who determine them. Who will vote for which candidate and why? Where are the voters? All of these questions and more were answered within my Human

Geography course and for that reason I now want to become a political strategist. This course combines math, science, history and even literature. There is literally something for everyone.

—Rachel Harris, 2012

AP human geography made me begin to see how things connect together in ways I had never noticed before. APHG has made me start to ask questions about everything I see around me. I also am beginning to understand how complex the world really is. Perhaps the most important thing about APHG is how relevant it is. No matter my career choice, the things I have learned in APHG will help me.

—Annabelle McNeill, 2015

Explore the World and the people in it. But first, take AP Human Geography. In this exciting and amazing class students will learn about the world we live in and the people on it. Everyone needs to be a part of this class to learn about other cultures and practices than what they see around them. Learn then Explore.

—Mitchell Kirsch, 2015

AP Human Geography contributes to the understanding of the how's and why's in communication and interaction across the globe, from the smallest scales to the largest scales. It shows what truly happens as countries are constantly doing business with the other countries surrounding them to strive socially, politically, and economically. Analyzing geographic concepts will be beneficial for any type of subject or study, as it makes you think "outside of the box," and through investigation of the neighboring locations and their properties, determine what it is that one place might have that another does not. Solving these kinds of mysteries and involving Geographical vocabulary while doing so helps you build your logical thinking for all classes or situations. AP Human Geography is valuable for any and all students looking to thrive in their education.

—Hunter Hermes, 2015

Part 1 Section 2: This Ain't Yo Momma's or Daddy's Geography class!

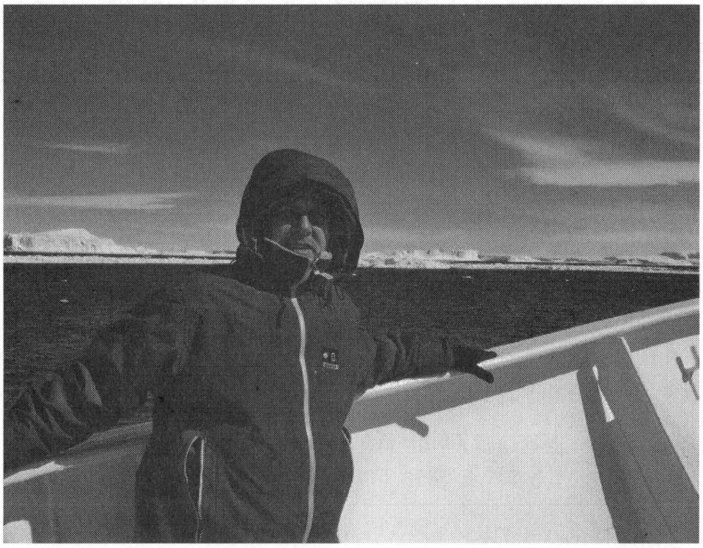

Paul Gray

Purpose

Your parents think they know what geography is, but life has changed a bit from when they were in school. Unfortunately, parents forget that their high school days were long ago in a world where there were no cell phones and Abraham Lincoln was still president (or for those of you with young parents perhaps Teddy Roosevelt).

The purpose of this section is to teach you what this class is—pretty simple and extremely important. We believe that the first step is to explain what the class isn't and then slowly give you definitions. So there are three parts to this section:

A. This Ain't Yo Momma's or Daddy's Geography!

B. What Is Geography?

C. What Is Human Geography?

Weddell Sea, Antarctica. Author Paul Gray visits one of the most remote places on the planet. Humans first set foot in Antarctica in 1895.

A. This Ain't Yo Momma's or Daddy's Geography!

Too many students assume they know what AP Human Geography is, but they really don't. Even more students take the class without really knowing what they've signed up for and wish they did know.

Sometimes students talk with their parents, and their parents tell them what they think the class is. Most parents think this class is something they took when they were in high school.

Despite what you might have thought, the following is a list of what this class is not:

This is not an AP coloring book class!

A lot of students assume that geography will be a coloring book class where they have to fill in countries or places with different colors and that's it. Yes, we will study maps! And yes, we will learn why different colors are used on maps. But if you thought you could get a credit in art by taking this class, you probably need to draw yourself a sad face right now.

This is not geography on Jeopardy!

You WON'T be memorizing capitals of countries, and you won't be quizzed on memorization. That's geography for *Jeopardy* and that's your daddy's (or granddaddy's) geography! Many elementary and high school geography courses focus on memorizing places. And while knowing where countries are and what their capitals are is great, this class goes far beyond mere memorization of places and creates a deep-rooted understanding of the world.

> We are here to tell you, *"This ain't yo Momma's or Daddy's geography!"*
> Your parents think they know what this class is. They don't!

This is not physical geography!

A physical geographer studies the Earth's natural phenomena such as climate, soil, plants, animals, and topography and looks for patterns and makes conclusions. Courses like Environmental Studies study these concepts.

A human geographer, while not ignoring the fact that deserts, rainfall, and the like affect the world, focuses on how peoples of the world structure their population, their cultures, and other activities. We don't study "what makes it rain"; rather, we study how PEOPLE deal with too much or too little rainfall as it relates to aspects of their lives ranging from their economic activities to their religious customs.

This is not a history class!

Although geographers use history and historians use geography, they differ fundamentally in their main approach to understanding events.

Historians use time as the framework of their courses. They study everything chronologically, starting at a certain time and moving forward. Essentially, historians ask "when" did something occur and then explain "why." Time lines are an essential component of a historical understanding. Geographers, in contrast to historians, use space as the framework of their courses. They study everything "spatially"; that is, they use space as the foundation.

Essentially, geographers are interested in "where" something is and "why" it is occurring in that particular location. (See the Where and Why There section on page 12 for more information.)

Some further thoughts:

1. Being good at memorizing capitals and countries won't hurt you.

The more you know about where places are in the world, the quicker you can make connections and the better you will understand concepts. It is easier to succeed with a strong mental map.

Knowing where countries and other places are on a map is like bringing a large plate to class. When the teacher serves up the food (information) in class, you'll get every last bit of it on your plate. And you'll know how to separate your broccoli from your potatoes. Mmmm ... knowledge. Tasty!

2. Being good at science won't hurt you.

Having a rock-solid foundation (get it!) in science (physical geography) provides a good background and connections for understanding the effects of humans on the planet. But again, our focus will be on humans and their impact on the environment, and not necessarily on the science behind the impact. In other words, we will not focus on what caused the hurricane or the earthquake, but on why so many people live in hazard zones.

3. Being good at history won't hurt you.

But just because you were good at history does not guarantee that you will do well in AP Human Geography. Many students struggle early in geography and say things like "but I usually do so well in history class."

Remember, the two courses are related, but they are different in their approaches. For history class, you need a chronological mind and you've developed that special skill over many years of history classes.

THINKING SPATIALLY!

Developing a spatial mind takes time for many students. We imagine that many of you are used to thinking historically and that you have a good chronological mind. However, this might be your first geography class, and so it might take time to get used to seeing information spatially.

But you need to think **spatially** in order to succeed. And we want you to be successful.

How about a quick lesson to begin your development of your spatial mind? All of you have no doubt seen the FedEx® logo? Here it is again.

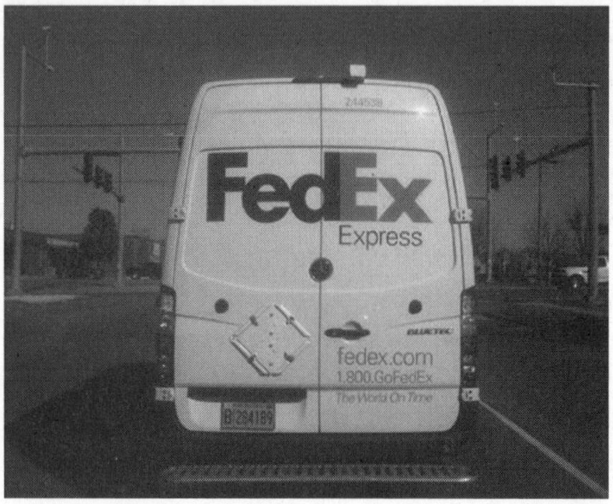

But have you ever noticed the arrow between the E and the x? If you haven't, look at the logo again.[5]

Now, try looking at the logo without seeing the arrow. You can't do it! This is what learning how to think spatially will do. You will see things that have been right in front of your eyes all along in a new way. This is the magic of thinking like a geographer.

THINKING SPATIALLY (PART 2)

Now how about this sign? It's just an interesting sign, right?

Paul T. Gray, Jr., Russellville High School

---

[5] From the work of John Stilgoe. Visit the link below to see more on how to interpret landscapes using Harvard professor John Stilgoe's work. CBS *60 Minutes* episode called "The Eyes Have It," January 5, 2004. http://www.cbsnews.com/stories/2003/12/31/60minutes/main590907.shtml?tag=mncol;lst;1

No, the sign is almost audibly shouting geographical components. Why does the sign exist? Why is there no liquor? Where is there a place that would have no liquor?

Once you learn how to think geographically, you'll see signs like this and you'll be forced to think about them! (See page 224 in your textbook on how to interpret this sign spatially. Do you have a hypothesis?)

FINAL THOUGHTS:
As we stated before, this could be your first geography class. Be patient. There will be terms that you will learn for the first time. Don't panic. Learning to think spatially might also take some time. Don't worry. Realize that this is a new experience and that with time you'll get it. Many students struggle in the beginning, but once they get it, they will never lose it—just like the FedEx logo.

WHERE AND WHY THERE: THE ESSENTIAL QUESTIONS OF AP HUMAN GEOGRAPHY

As the saying goes, "You are nowhere without geography!" The best advice for you throughout the entire year is to learn to always ask "where" and "why there." So whether you have read a section of notes, looked at a map, or studied a chart, stop yourself and ask yourself the "where" and "why there" questions.

Here are the basic steps:

- Think about **where** the pattern exists.
- Look for **where** the pattern doesn't exist.
- Then start asking yourself **why there**.

Both are challenging skills, but admittedly figuring out the "why there" can be a great adventure. Students (and teachers) ponder all the different possibilities as to why a pattern exists. Sometimes the answer is simple, and as the year goes on and you learn more about the world, you will start to make more connections faster than your Internet speed.

B. What Is Geography?

By now, we hope that you have begun to shape an idea of what AP Human Geography isn't (and have gotten a little bit of an idea of what it is). But let's take a step back. Perhaps the best way to begin to understand "What is AP Human Geography?" is to begin with "What is geography?".

And the best approach to that is to start with a few definitions.

Geography:

- is the scientific study of the Earth's surface.
- studies the interactions between people and their physical environments.
- focuses on the locational and spatial variations of phenomena, both human and nonhuman (so-called natural or physical/biological).
- is descriptive, that is, describes a phenomenon (an occurrence), where it is located, and how it is related to other phenomena (occurrences).
- identifies regions (again, both human/cultural and physical/biological regions).
- describes, analyzes, explains, and interprets.

Charles Fuller, former geography professor at Triton College, has used the following description of geography in his course syllabi:

> Geography is the systematic study of the spatial patterns of all phenomena on or near the Earth's surface. Its primary methodology is spatial analysis, which asks two basic questions: **where** are things located (spatial), and why are they located where they are (analysis—**why there**). Its primary tool of communication is the map.

Stop for a second. Notice the use of **"the words where** and **why there"** in the definition. Remember, "Where" and "Why There" are the essential questions in the course!

Now, let's see how the idea of spatial analysis is described using those two questions. "Where" gives us the spatial part, and "Why There" gives us the analysis. One other word worth taking note of is "pattern." Geographers scan maps to look for patterns or instances of phenomena (occurrences). Where is this occurring? Where isn't it occurring? Is there a pattern? Why does this pattern exist?

To get a better understanding of how geography works, please read the following essay about Chicago and geography.

Defining Geography: What Is It? What Does It Mean?

By: James Marran

Many people perceive geography as simply an exercise in place location. That means being able to answer a single question about a place: Where is it? If, for example, Chicago is identified as a city in northeastern Illinois on the southwestern shore of Lake Michigan, that information has indeed answered the "Where is it?" question. To be even more accurate, data on the city's latitudinal and longitudinal coordinates could be given showing it at 41°49'N, 87°37'W.

Even though such identifiers about Chicago's location are accurate, they bring the inquirer only to the threshold of really getting the total "geographic" picture because there are other more important and more interesting questions to pose and answer about places. Chicago becomes far more meaningful when it is understood in the context of the answers to these questions:

- Why is it where it is?
- How did it get there?
- What does it look like?
- Where is it in relation to other places?
- Why did it grow so large?
- How does it interact with other places?
- How is it connected to other places in its region, its country, its continent, and the world?

Learning the answers to these questions begins to give Chicago dimension and meaning since they identify both its physical (natural) and human (cultural) features. They also provide a context for studying the spatial characteristics of the city by making clear both its site (its physical setting) and its situation (its location in relation to other places). More importantly, the interaction between Chicago's physical and cultural features helps explain its role as an immensely diverse urban magnet that for almost two centuries has drawn people from across the world to live and work in its neighborhoods and the hinterland (i.e., suburbs) beyond.

Photographs and maps showing the tracks that lace the city's rail yards like so many scrimshaw etchings and mile-long runways accommodating thousands of flights daily at O'Hare International Airport reveal a tapestry of transportation networks moving people, goods, ideas, and services to and from all corners of the Earth. And the communications aerials atop the Sears (Willis) Tower and the Hancock Building in the central business district (downtown) send images and words that inform, entertain, and challenge people around the globe. As a manufacturing core and marketplace, Chicago provides a commercial function that helps make the economy of the United States the world's largest and strongest.

Certainly a list inventorying the city's role that derives from its location could go on and on, but the point is clear. Wherever a place is only marks the beginning of giving it definition and establishing its importance among other places. By examining the spatial aspects of a place's location and how the people living there function and make their living confirm that geography is not so much about the memorization of facts but also asking questions, solving problems and making informed decisions about the physical and human complexities of the planet.

So, why is Chicago a large city in the United States? It is safe to say that it is because of its geography. But remember that its geography encompasses both its physical setting (an inland port city) and its human features: cultural, political, and economic. As a result of those combined geographic forces, Chicago became a transportation hub (center), a center for manufacturing, and a dominant city in the United States. And truly, this essay helps us bridge the gap between "What Is Geography?" and "What is Human Geography?"

C. What Is Human Geography?

Human Geography is one of the major divisions of geography; the spatial analysis of human population, its cultures, activities, and landscapes.

—Fouberg, Murphy, and de Blij 9th edition

Not a bad definition at all! So let's break it down:

- We know what geography is, so we're off to a good start!
- We have looked at the terms *spatial* and *analysis* already.
- The rest of the definition is pretty simple to understand.

But let's expand on the definition so that we can get a really good understanding about what you will be studying in class.

Using the spatial perspective, Human Geographers look at ***where*** something occurs, search for patterns, and span most of the social studies disciplines to answer the ***why there*** question.

Therefore, in the end, students in Human Geography will study history, religion, politics, economics, sociology, and other social studies subjects. Geography (through maps, charts, etc.) shows us where something occurs. Then we work with the other social studies subjects when they help us answer the ***why there*** question.

Human Geography covers all of the social studies subjects under the sun. If only there was a visual to illustrate the importance of Human Geography. And you've probably guessed it: There is such a graphic:

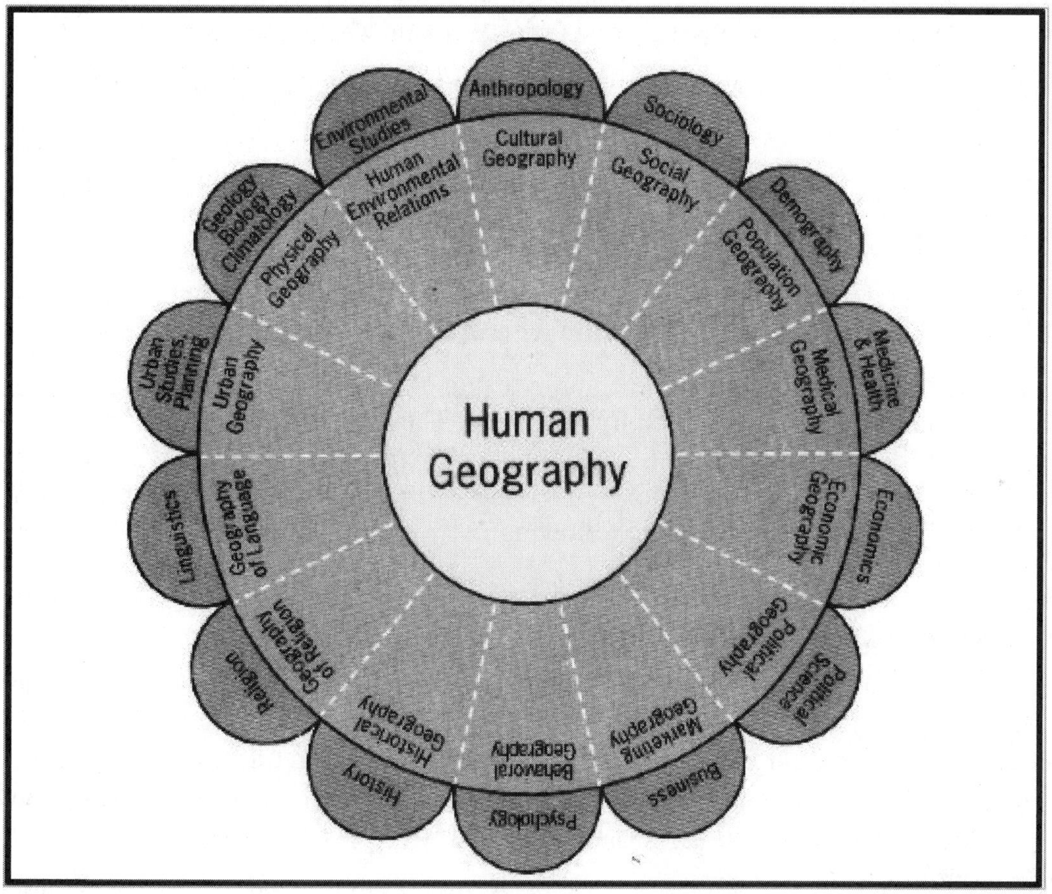

In the end, Human Geography provides the foundation for understanding fundamental similarities and differences between people culturally, politically, economically, and socially through a spatial perspective. It is a capstone course that will help you in other classes in your academic career. In fact, we like to think that just like the globe it will make you well rounded.

Let's recap. You should now know what Human Geography is not; you should have a sense of what geography is; and finally you should understand what, specifically, Human Geography is. But just in case you need some more detail, we've included a small sampling of topics covered in Human Geography:

- Students will study the conflict between Spanish speakers in California and English speakers on one scale, but they will also learn about other conflicts such as the one between Flemish and French speakers in Belgium.
- Students will learn about where their food comes from and how it is produced. Did you know your strawberry shake from a fast-food restaurant does not have one strawberry in it? It does, however, have over 45 chemicals that make it taste like strawberries.[6]
- Students will study transportation network patterns and the impact the Federal Highway Act of 1956 had on the development of the United States, comparing it with the lack of development of a transcontinental railroad in Africa and its impact on the economy.
- Students will study the conflict between secularism and religion in the world today, how Islam got to Indonesia, how Confucianism blended with Buddhism in China, and how Catholicism and Protestantism didn't blend in Northern Ireland.
- Students will study how demographic shifts will change American politics in the next couple of decades. For example, Hispanics will become the majority in the United States by 2040 or so. Whites will be the largest minority followed by African Americans. How will this change electoral politics? To what states will federal monies flow during and after these demographic shifts? What policies will be changed?

Summary: The Five Major Goals of AP Human Geography

The people who designed the AP Human Geography exam based the content on *five college-level goals* that build on the National Geography Standards. These five goals truly describe what this course is about and what skills you should acquire after completing the class. As the College Board Course Description booklet points out, if you successfully complete the course and do well on the exam, you should be able to do the following:

Interpret maps and analyze geospatial data.

Geography is concerned with the ways in which patterns on Earth's surface reflect and influence physical and human processes. As such, maps and geographic information systems (GIS) are fundamental to the discipline, and learning to use and think about them is critical to geographical literacy. The goal is achieved when students learn to use maps and geospatial data to pose and solve problems, and when they learn to think critically about what is revealed and what is hidden in different maps and GIS applications.

Understand and explain the implications of associations and networks among phenomena in places.

Geography looks at the world from a spatial perspective, seeking to understand the changing spatial organization and material character of Earth's surface. One of the critical advantages of a spatial perspective is the attention it focuses on how phenomena are related to one another in

[6] Eric Schlosser, *Fast Food Nation: The Dark Side of the American Meal* (New York: HarperCollins Books, 2002), pp. 125–126.

particular places. Students should thus learn not just to recognize and interpret patterns but to assess the nature and significance of the relationships among phenomena that occur in the same place, and to understand how cultural values, political regulations, and economic constraints work together to create particular landscapes.

Recognize and interpret the relationships among patterns and processes at different scales of analysis.

Geographical analysis requires a sensitivity to scale, not just as a spatial category but as a framework for understanding how events and processes at different scales influence one another. Thus students should understand that the phenomena they are studying at one scale (e.g., local) may well be influenced by processes and developments at other scales (e.g., global, regional, national, state or provincial). They should then look at processes operating at multiple scales when seeking explanations of geographic patterns and arrangements.

Define regions and evaluate the regionalization process.

Geography is concerned not simply with describing patterns but with analyzing how they came about and what they mean. Students should see regions as objects of analysis and exploration and move beyond simply locating and describing regions to considering how and why they come into being and what they reveal about the changing character of the world in which we live.

Characterize and analyze changing interconnections among places.

At the heart of a geographical perspective is a concern with the ways in which events and processes operating in one place can influence those operating at other places. Thus students should view places and patterns not in isolation but in terms of their spatial and functional relationship with other places and patterns. Moreover, they should strive to be aware that those relationships are constantly changing, and they should understand how and why change occurs.

Topics in AP Human Geography

AP Human Geography covers seven major topics throughout the year. The following lists the topics in the order assigned by the College Board (please note that teachers sometimes will cover these topics in a different order):

	Content Area (Topic)	*Percentage Goals for Exam*
I.	Geography: Its Nature and Perspectives	5–10%
II.	Population	13–17%
III.	Cultural Patterns and Processes	13–17%
IV.	Political Organization of Space	13–17%
V.	Agriculture and Rural Land Use	13–17%
VI.	Industrialization and Economic Development	13–17%
VII.	Cities and Urban Land Use	13–17%

The percentages mark the range of multiple-choice questions that will be on the AP exam from each section.

Part 1 Section 3: How to read my textbook (or how this workbook saved my grade)

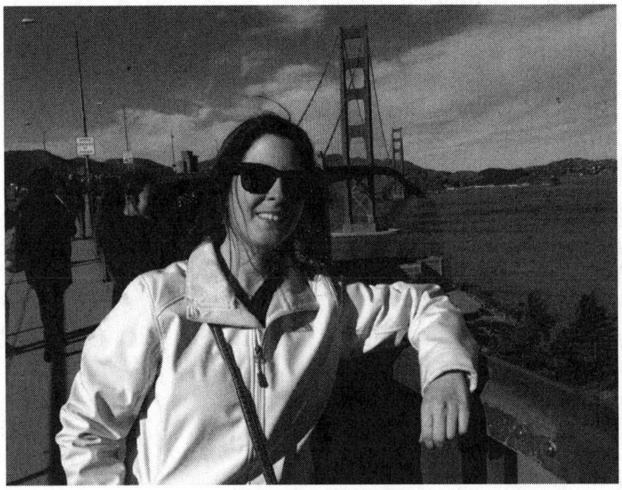

Paris Meymand

Purpose

The purpose of this section is to teach you how to read your *Human Geography: People, Place, and Culture* textbook. Remember, this is a college textbook, and there is a ton of new vocabulary flying off the pages. Our goal in this workbook is to make your learning easier and to make the textbook accessible.

So here are the three sections:

A. Learning to Read Again: SMH (Smack my Head)

B. How Is a Chapter Designed?

C. The Five Steps to Chapter Success

Golden Gate Bridge, San Francisco. Author Parisa Meymand at the most photographed bridge in the world and an engineering marvel when built in 1937.

A. Learning to Read Again: SMH (Shake my head)

Yes, you know how to read. But let's face it, these days for many of you it comes in the form of text messages—AYK. A whole language and skill are involved in being able to read text messages. In fact, you developed that skill over time. However, thanks to your parents' generous cell phone plan and several crises at school, you worked and developed that skill and became better at writing and reading text messages. Who knew that texting was a skill-LOL.

Learning how to read a college-level geography text is something that will take some time getting used to. OMG!

For many of you, this is your first Advanced Placement course. Taking a college-level course requires understanding a very comprehensive and often nuanced vocabulary.

> Translation for you: There are a lot of big words that you might be unfamiliar with, and there are sometimes similar words that have slightly different meanings.

In addition, this might be your first geography class or perhaps your last geography class was in elementary school. So, you are probably unfamiliar with geographic thinking; therefore, reading a geography book will be challenging.

The rest of this section is accordingly set up to help you become a more skilled reader of your textbook. We will go through the format of each chapter. We will also give you reading tools that we have created that force you to be a more careful reader. We believe that by the end of the year you probably won't need to use every tool because you will have trained yourself to do it instinctively.

Remember, we're JHO and this is FYI. You could DIY, but you probably would FDGB!

> Translation for your teacher: Remember, we're <u>just helping out</u> and this is <u>for your information</u>. You could <u>do it yourself</u>, but you probably would <u>fall down—go boom</u>.

B. How Is Each Chapter Designed?

The best way to prepare to read your textbook is to have an idea of how each chapter is designed. Your textbook has a wonderful format, and once you get a feel for it, the better you will anticipate what is coming up next and make better connections.

Here is the basic structure of every chapter:

*1. **Field Note** (The Introduction)*

Your textbook starts out with wonderful personal primary source accounts about the area of geography you will be studying. One of the three authors reflects on a place he or she has studied and connects it to what you will be studying. Through pictures and vivid descriptions of a particular location, you are transported to that location (without ever leaving home). Typically, once a particular location is described, the scale is changed and the focus becomes more global. Sometimes maps are included to give you additional data to help you better understand.

The purpose is to hopefully create excitement and interest, but at the very least to provide a "discussion-style" reading for you—to give you the feel that the author is talking just to you.

Sure, sometimes big vocabulary words are used in the Field Note, but generally the idea is to give you a sense of place and a sense of the importance of the chapter you are going to begin.

We often find that students will only glance through the Field Note. We feel this is not only unfortunate but unwise.

2. Key Questions List (How will the chapter be divided?)

After the Field Note, the next part of the chapter presents a list of Key Questions. The Key Questions are actually the titles to the sections of the chapter, and there are typically four or five in every chapter.

We creatively offer you these sections in the form of a question because the question should immediately trigger to you what you are about to read. For instance, in Chapter 3, one of the Key Questions is "Why do people migrate?" Well, if you don't know why people migrate, you should know a lot about it by the end of the section.

We also like to list all the Key Questions right after the Field Note. This should give you a greater understanding of the overall goals of the chapter.

Again, we think many students glance through these Key Questions without giving them much thought. And again, we think this is unwise.

3. A Key Question (A section in a chapter)

In the next part of a chapter, you specifically begin to read a specific section that is the Key Question we previously mentioned. You need to understand a few things before you begin reading a Key Question.

For starters, not all Key Questions are the same length. So it is important to look at the length of the section before you begin reading. This will better prepare you for how long you will need to focus.

The other things you need to know are as follow:

- ***Key Questions*** are denoted in **BOLD** and are set in ALL CAPS.
- ***Subsections*** within the Key Question are denoted in **green and in boldface.** Subsections are typically 4 to 10 paragraphs long.
- Key terms (which are called ***Geographic Concepts***) will be in **bold** as you read. Please note that you should be able to understand a Geographic Concept within the context of the reading. However, if you are unable to do so, you can go to the glossary in the Appendix of the book for a full definition.
- Each Key Question ends with a ***Thinking Geographically*** feature. Typically, this feature gets you to consider your own world and geography. It also encourages you to think about geography in your space.

4. ***Maps, Photos, Charts, and Graphs*** *(the Base of Geography)*

Throughout every chapter there are a series of photographs, maps, charts, and graphs. All of these visual aids are extremely important. We know that in other textbooks many of you see a picture or map and go "Hooray!" Your thought is that you can skip over the visual and therefore have less to read. But remember, geography is a spatial class and is therefore one in which being a visual learner is important.

> All of the visuals contain information that is important and can be assessed on a test. A picture can really give you a sense of place, a sense of the human element in geography.

Right now, imagine you are in India. What would that picture look like? That picture could be different for all of us depending on where we are in India: near a sacred site, in downtown Bangalore, or in a rural rice village. However, those images are filled with an imprint of technology, culture, and human interaction with the environment. And they differ throughout the world.

Charts and graphs do a great job of presenting data to you in a visual way, making it easy to compare and contrast information. For instance, in your textbook on p. 46-47, there are Age–Sex Population Pyramids for poorer countries and for wealthier countries. These images do a great job of visually demonstrating the contrast in these countries' populations.

Maps are probably the most essential visual used in the textbook. In fact, Appendix A in your textbook gives you a crash course on the importance of maps. It is something we encourage you to read at the beginning of the year.

And while maps are important in a geography class, world maps are the kings. Every chapter in your textbook has at least one world map (Chapter 1 has four).

> World maps are the cool kid in class, the smart kid in school, the best musician in the band, and the varsity athlete all rolled into one. And of course, they are very attractive.

And whether it is love at first sight or a gradual process of getting to know the world maps and learning to appreciate them, you will become attached to them.

At the same time, we are aware that this might be your first time having to read a map for deep meaning. We also know that you might look at a map for a while and think you've learned the information, but you might have missed a portion of the information.

5. Guest Field Note

Occasionally, a picture will be accompanied by another Field Note. Just like the Field Note at the beginning of the chapter, this field note is a snapshot of a particular place. Again, it gives you another opportunity to see the application of a concept in the real world. You should always include these additional Field Notes in your notes.

6. Summary

Each chapter concludes with a summary. This is truly a great way to make sure you have understood the overarching framework of the chapter. If you read the summary and are confused, then you need to go back and reread the chapter. And even if you understand the summary, that does not guarantee you success on a test. Remember, the summary is a framework or a general understanding of the chapter. In a college-level course, details are going to be key.

We believe that if you've taken notes throughout the chapter, then the summary should make sense. We also believe that you will have enough detail in your notes to do well on tests.

7. Geographic Concepts

One of the last parts of the chapter is a list of all the key vocabulary terms that you need to know. These were all the bold words in your textbook, and there are definitions for all of these words in your glossary. It is probably a good idea to look at this list after studying and see if you can recall the term without looking up the definition. If you can, you've got it! If not, you need to go to your notes, reread the definition, or go back to the text.

8. Learn More Online and Watch It Online

The final part of the chapter gives you an opportunity to explore the geographic topic on your own and in more detail. Specific websites are given to you for further research.

C. The Five Steps to Chapter Success Explained

Okay, now you know the format for each chapter. We have created "The Five Steps to Chapter Success" for each chapter. We believe that if you follow these steps, you will have a much better understanding and a better chance for success on the tests.

The Five Steps to Chapter Success

Step 1: Read the Chapter Summary below and preview the Key Questions.
Step 2: Complete the Pre-Reading Activity (PRA) for this chapter.
Step 3: Read the chapter and complete the guided worksheet.
Step 4: Study the world maps and take our "Map It!" quiz.
Step 5: Take a Practice AP-style practice quiz over the whole chapter.

As you get into each chapter, the steps should be pretty clear. However, because this is a geography class, Step 4 is a VERY IMPORTANT STEP that will help you improve your reading of maps and your understanding of geography.

The Purpose of Step 4 (Learning how to REALLY read World Maps)

The purpose of Step 4 is to make sure you are reading the maps for detail. It is a very important skill for a geography class.

World maps are like elephants. They're big, tough, and hard to sink your teeth into—not that you would want to eat an elephant. But think for a second: What if you had to eat an elephant? How would you do it? Hopefully, you would consider going slowly and eating it bit by bit.

Staring at a world map can be as overwhelming as thinking about consuming a whole elephant. The trick with both is to consume a map piece by piece instead of swallowing it whole.

When you see a world map on population, it's easy to pick up overall information, just like it's easy to see that an elephant is gray. But the trick of learning how to read a world map effectively is learning how to divide it into parts and finding patterns on a smaller scale. In essence, it amounts to "eating" the map bit by bit.

We suggest you divide the world into 12 different regions (also known as realms) based on human/cultural elements to help you better organize the information from a world map. These regions are as follows:

1. Europe
2. Russia (with Armenia, Azerbaijan, and Georgia)
3. North America
4. Middle America *
5. South America *
6. Subsaharan Africa
7. North Africa/Southwest Asia
8. South Asia
9. East Asia
10. Southeast Asia
11. Austral (Australia, New Zealand)
12. South Pacific Islands*

*Please note: There is no one way to divide the world up into different cultural regions. In fact, many geographers combine Middle America and South America into one region, naming it Latin America. Also, the South Pacific Islands are small in population and size. Therefore, many times the region is seen as less important from a global perspective.

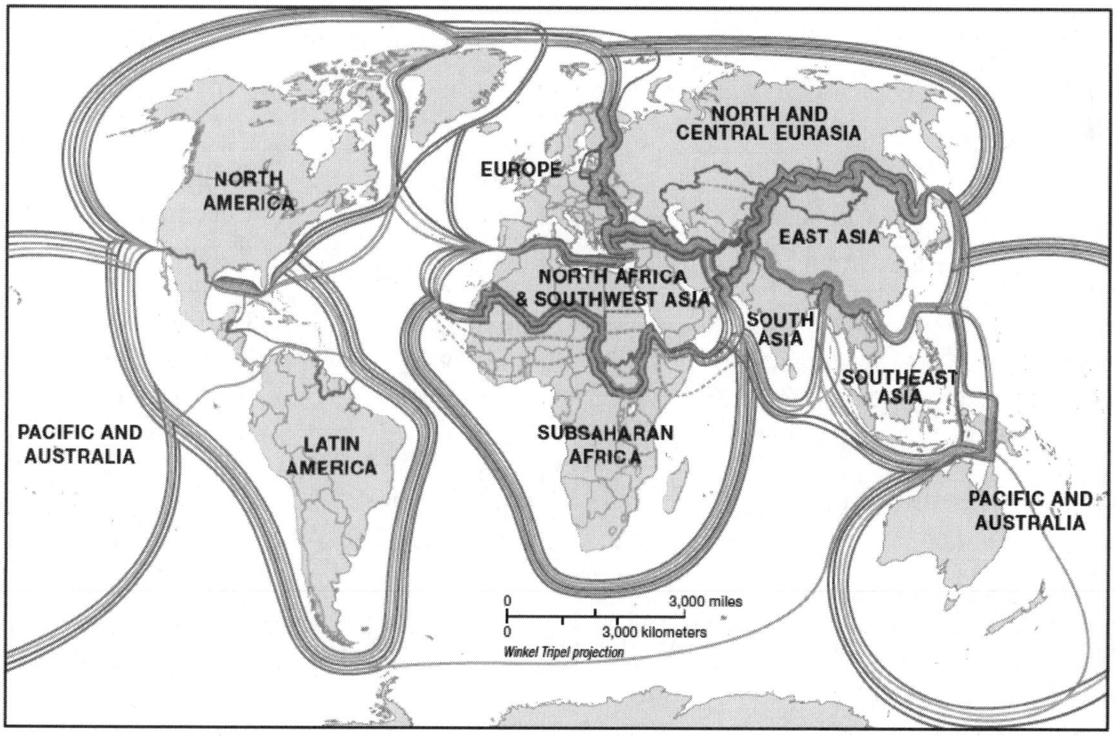

We have provided you with a list of the major countries from each of these regions on the next few pages. You will see these countries on the world maps used in your textbook. Small countries (microstates) such as Andorra or Seychelles are not included in this list because of their small scale, but the country list includes the major countries in the world.

On pages 24–26, we have provided you with a graphic organizer for the world maps. We think this sheet should be filled out every time you read a world map in your textbook. Additional organizers are on the Wiley Student Companion Website and are available for you to download and print.

The organizer includes a list of each region and space in between so that you can take notes. There are additional prompts that give you an opportunity to comment on patterns you see. These sheets should help you take the time to read world maps slowly and effectively.

Just remember: You need to look at a map from both a general and a specific perspective. You need to search for patterns. And do remember ***where*** and ***why***! When you take notes on a map, think about the following:

- Where is "it" occurring?
- Where is "it" not occurring?
- Is there a pattern?
- Why is there a pattern?

HUMAN GEOGRAPHY: WORLD REGIONS AND WORLD MAPS

Below is a list of the major countries located in the 12 world regions on a world map.

1 Europe

Albania	Austria	Belarus	Belgium
Bosnia	Bulgaria	Croatia	Czech Republic
Denmark	Estonia	Finland	France
Germany	Greece	Hungary	Iceland
Ireland	Italy	Kosovo	Latvia
Liechtenstein	Lithuania	Luxembourg	Macedonia
Malta	Moldova	Montenegro	Netherlands
Norway	Poland	Portugal	Romania
Serbia	Slovakia	Slovenia	Spain
Sweden	Switzerland	Ukraine	United Kingdom

2 Russia and Caucasus states

Russia	Armenia	Azerbaijan	Georgia

3 North America

Canada	United States

4 Middle America and Caribbean

Belize	Costa Rica	Cuba	Dominican Republic
El Salvador	Guatemala	Haiti	Honduras
Jamaica	Mexico	Nicaragua	Panama
Puerto Rico (U.S.)			

5 South America

Argentina Bolivia	Brazil	Chile	Colombia
Ecuador	French Guiana (France)	Guyana	Paraguay
Peru	Suriname	Uruguay	Venezuela

6 Subsaharan Africa

Angola	Benin	Botswana	Burkina Faso
Burundi	Cameroon	Central African Republic	Chad
Congo	Comoros	Dem. Rep. of Congo	Ethiopia
Djibouti	Equatorial Guinea	Eritrea	Guinea
Gabon	Gambia	Ghana	Lesotho
Guinea-Bissau	Ivory Coast	Kenya	Mali
Liberia	Madagascar	Malawi	Niger
Mauritius	Mozambique	Namibia	Sierra Leone
Nigeria	Rwanda	Senegal	Swaziland
Somalia	South Africa	South Sudan	Zambia
Tanzania	Togo	Uganda	Zimbabwe

7 North Africa and Southwest Asia

Afghanistan	Algeria	Bahrain	Egypt
Iran	Iraq	Israel	Jordan
Kazakhstan	Kuwait	Kyrgyzstan	Lebanon
Libya	Morocco	Oman	Qatar
Saudi Arabia	Sudan	Syria	Tajikistan
Tunisia	Turkey	Turkmenistan	United Arab Emirates
Uzbekistan	Western Sahara	Yemen	

8 South Asia

Bangladesh	India	Pakistan	Sri Lanka
Bhutan	Nepal		

9 East Asia

China	Mongolia	North Korea	South Korea
Japan	North Korea	Taiwan (PRC)	

10 Southeast Asia

Brunei	Cambodia	East Timor	Indonesia
Laos	Malaysia	Myanmar (Burma)	Philippines
Singapore	Thailand	Vietnam	

11 Austral Region

Australia	New Zealand

12 South Pacific Islands

Fiji	New Caledonia	Papua New Guinea
Solomon Islands	Vanuati	

WORLD REGION MAP ORGANIZER

Student Name ______________________________ **Chapter** __________
Title (Map): ______________________________ **pages** __________

Think Spatially: Look at the map and find patterns that seem to exist in general.
List general facts/patterns found on this map:

1. ______________________________
____
2. ______________________________
____
3. ______________________________
____
4. ______________________________
____
5. ______________________________
____

Think Regionally: Now, focus on a particular region and list key details from the map for each region (bullet points are fine).

1 Europe

2 Russia

3 North America

4 Middle America

5 South America

6 Subsarahan Africa

7 North Africa and Southwest Asia

8 South Asia

9 East Asia

10 Southeast Asia

11 Austral (Australia, New Zealand)

12 South Pacific Islands

Summary

Your textbook is written at a college level that can be extremely challenging. The purpose of the rest of this part of the workbook is to make that reading easier by providing you a step-by-step process on reading the chapter.

We know that this process works. We also know that it might seem like more time at first. However, if you complete these steps, you shouldn't have to go back and reread the chapter. Everything is set up for you.

Also, by following these steps, you naturally become a better reader.

Once more, here are the Five Steps to Chapter Success:

Step 1: Read the Chapter Summary below and preview the Key Questions.

Step 2: Complete the Pre-Reading Activity (PRA) for this chapter.

Step 3: Read the chapter and complete the guided worksheet.

Step 4: Study the world maps, and take our "Map It!" quiz.

Step 5: Take a Practice AP-style practice quiz over the whole chapter.

Part 2: Understanding Your Textbook

Purpose

The purpose of this Part of the workbook is truly the WORK-part of the book. You will go through "The Five Steps to Success" for every chapter.

Since this is a college textbook, this next part of the book helps you read it for understanding and check your understanding with multiple-choice questions. You really know if you know the material after going through the Five Steps to Success:

Step 1: Read the Chapter Summary below and preview the Key Questions.

Step 2: Complete the Pre-Reading Activity (PRA) for this chapter.

Step 3: Read the chapter and complete the guided worksheet.

Step 4: Study the World Maps and take our "Map It!" Quiz

Step 5: Take a Practice AP-style practice quiz.

Grant Park, Chicago. This picture illustrates the balance, need, and tension that exists in creating green space in urban environments.

CHAPTER 1:
INTRODUCTION TO HUMAN GEOGRAPHY

Name: ______________________________ **Period** __________ **Date** __________

Chapter Title: ____

Chapter # ______________________________ **Pgs.** __________ **to** __________

The Five Steps to Chapter Success

Step 1: Read the Chapter Summary below and preview the Key Questions.
Step 2: Complete the Pre-Reading Activity (PRA) for this chapter.
Step 3: Read the chapter and complete the guided worksheet.
Step 4: Study the World Maps and take our "Map It!" Quiz
Step 5: Take a Practice AP-style practice quiz.

STEP 1: Chapter Summary and Key Questions

Chapter Summary

Our study of human geography will analyze people and places and explain how they interact across space and time to create our world. Chapters 2 and 3 lay the basis for our study of human geography by looking at where people live. Chapters 4–7 focus on aspects of culture and how people use culture and identity to make sense of themselves in their world. The remaining chapters examine how people have created a world in which they function economically, politically, and socially, and show how their activities in those realms re-create themselves and their world.

Key Questions

Field Note: Awakening to World Hunger	p. 1–4
1. What is human geography?	p. 5
2. What are geographic questions?	p. 5–11
3. Why do geographers use maps, and what do maps tell us?	p. 11–18
4. Why are geographers concerned with scale and connectedness?	p. 18–26
5. What are geographic concepts, and how are they used in answering geographic questions?	p. 26–27

Step 2: Pre-Reading Activity (PRA)

1. Which key question is the longest? Which one is the shortest?

Key Question	# of Pages

2. After looking over the Key Questions, looking through the outline and reading the chapter summary, write a few sentences about what you expect to learn in general in this chapter.

3. How many world maps are there in this chapter? _____ (Go to the Student Companion Website and print out organizers for help.)

4. Read the Field Note introduction of the chapter and list three specific facts you learned.

6. Go to the end of the chapter and look at the Geographic Concepts. Create a list of terms you think you know and terms you need to know.

I THINK I KNOW	I NEED TO LEARN

Step 3: Chapter 1 Guided Worksheet

Directions: As you read the chapter, fill in the blanks on the guided worksheet.

FIELD NOTE—AWAKENING TO WORLD HUNGER

1. When I visited ___________ in Eastern Africa, I drove from Masai Mara to Kericho and noticed that nearly all of the agricultural fields I could see were planted with __________ or ________.
2. The major causes of malnourishment are __________ (inability to pay for food), the failure of food distribution systems, and ____________ and _____________ practices that favor some groups over others.
3. _______ ________ people subsist on the equivalent of ______ dollars a day, and many in the vast ___________ encircling some of the world's largest cities must pay rent to landlords who own the plots on which their shacks are built. Too little is left for food, and it is the __________ who suffer most.
4. As part of an increasingly globalized economy, Kenya suffers from the complexities of ___________. With foreign corporations owning Kenya's best lands, a globalized economy that thrives on_________ ___________, tiny farms that are unproductive, and a gendered legal system that disenfranchises the agricultural labor force and disempowers the caregivers of the country's children, _________ has multiple factors contributing to poverty and malnutrition in the country.

WHAT IS HUMAN GEOGRAPHY?

5. Human geographers study __________ and places. The field of _________ _________ focuses on how people make places, how we organize space and society, how we interact with each other in places and across space, and how we make sense of others and ourselves in our localities, regions and the world.
6. Advances in communication and _________ _______ are making places and people more _______________.
7. ___________ all over the world are fundamentally affected by globalization. _____________ is a set of processes that are increasing interactions, deepening relationships, and accelerating interdependence across national borders.
8. Globalizing processes occur at the world_________; these processes bypass country __________ and include global financial markets and global environmental change.
9. No place on Earth is __________ by people. Each _________ we see is affected by and created by people, and each place reflects the ___________ of the people in that place over time.

WHAT ARE GEOGRAPHIC QUESTIONS?

10. Human geography is the study of the ________ and material characteristics of the human-made places and people, and ___________ _____________ is the study of spatial and material characteristics of physical environment.

11. Geographer Marvin Mikesell once gave a shorthand definition of geography as the "________of _________."
12. Whether they are ________ geographers or ____________ geographers, virtually all geographers are interested in the ________ arrangement of places and phenomena, how they are laid out, organized, and arranged on Earth, and how they appear on the landscape.
13. Mapping the ________ ____________of a phenomenon can be the first step to understanding it. By looking at a _______ of how something is distributed across space, a geographer can raise questions about how the arrangement came about, what processes create and sustain the particular distributions or ____________, and what relationships exist among different places and things.
14. In medical geography, mapping the distribution of a ____________ is the first step to finding its cause. In 1854, Dr.________ _________, a noted anesthesiologist in London, mapped cases of ______________ in London's Soho District.
15. ______________ is an ancient disease associated with diarrhea and dehydration. It was confined to ________ until the beginning of the nineteenth century. In 1816 it spread to China, Japan, East Africa, and Mediterranean Europe in the first of several ______________, that is, worldwide outbreaks of the disease.
16. A cholera outbreak in the slums of _________, ____________, in January 1991 became a fast-spreading ______________(regional outbreak of a disease) that touched every country in the Americas, infected more than 1 million people, and killed over 10,000 in the region.
17. Geographic literacy involves much more than ________________ places on a map. Place locations are to ________________ what dates are to __________.
18. Human geographers employ a ___________ _______________as they study a multitude of phenomena ranging from political elections and urban shantytowns to gay neighborhoods and folk music.
19. The National Geographic Society published its findings in 1986, introducing the ________ ___________of geography: location, human–environment interactions, ________, place, and _______________.
20. The first theme, ___________, highlights how the geographical position of people and things on Earth's surface affects what happens and why.
21. The second of the five themes concerns _________________________interactions. The third theme of geography is the ___________. The fourth theme is represented by the seemingly simple word __________.
22. People develop a ___________ ___ __________by infusing a place with meaning and emotion, by remembering important events that occurred in a place, or by labeling a place with a certain character. We also develop ________________ ___ ____________where we have never been through books, movies, stories, and pictures.
23. The fifth theme, ______________, refers to the mobility of people, goods, and ideas. Movement is an expression of the interconnectedness of __________. Spatial ____________ between places depends on the distances (the measured physical space between two places) among places, the _______________ (the ease of reaching one location from another) of places, and the transportation and communication ______________ (the degree of linkage between locations in a network) among places.

24. Human geographers are particularly concerned with the __________ ____________, the visible imprint of human activity on the landscape. The geographer whose name is most closely identified with this concept is former University of California at Berkeley professor ________ ___________.
25. Cultural landscapes have layers of impressions from compounded years of ________ activity. Imprints made by a ____________ of occupants, whose impacts are layered one on _____ of the other, were described as a cultural landscape of sequent occupance in 1929 by Derwent Whittlesey.

WHY DO GEOGRAPHERS USE MAPS, AND WHAT DO MAPS TELL US?

26. __________ are incredibly powerful tools in geography, and ______________, which is the art and science of making maps, is as old as geography itself. ____________ maps show locations of places and geographic features. ______________ maps tell stories, typically showing the degree of some attribute or the movement of a geographic phenomenon.
27. Reference maps accurately show the ______________ _____________of places, using a coordinate system that allows for the precise plotting of where on Earth something is.
28. Establishment of the satellite-based _________ ______________ ____________(GPS) allows us to locate features on Earth with extraordinary accuracy. ____________is a popular hobby based on the use of GPS.
29. ____________ _______________describes the location of a place in relation to other human and physical features.
30. ____________ locations do not change, but ________ locations are constantly modified and change over time.
31. We all carry maps in our minds of places we have been and places we have merely heard of; these are called _________ _________.
32. Our mental maps of the places within our _____________ __________, the places we travel to routinely in our rounds of _______ activity, are more accurate and detailed than our mental maps of places where we have _________ been.
33. All maps _________ the world. ______________maps help us see general trends, but we cannot see all cases of a given phenomenon.
34. Geographers monitor Earth from a distance, using ________ ____________technology.

WHY ARE GEOGRAPHERS CONCERNED WITH SCALE AND CONNECTEDNESS?

35. Geographers study patterns at a variety of scales including __________, ____________, ____________and ______________.
36. _________ has two meanings in geography: the first is the ____________ on a map compared to the distance on Earth, and the second is the _________ ___________of something. When we refer to scale we are using the __________ of these definitions.
37. A __________constitutes an area that shares similar characteristics and as a whole is distinct from other regions. Geographers define regions as ___________, ____________, or _________________.
38. A ___________ ___________ is marked by visible uniformity or a shared trait.

39. A ________________ ___________ is defined by a particular set of activities or interactions that occur within it.

40. Regions may be ______________, intellectual constructs that help people order their knowledge and understanding of the world. Each person carries perceptual regions in their mind based on accumulated ________________ of regions and cultures.

41. Cultural geographer _________ ___________ tackled the complex task of defining and delimiting the _____________ regions of the United States and southern Canada.

42. __________ refers not only to the music, literature, and arts of a society but to all the other features of its way of life: prevailing modes of ________ ; routine living habits; _______ preferences; the _____________ of houses and public buildings; the layout of fields and farms; and systems of education, government, and law. Culture is an _________________ term that identifies not only the whole tangible lifestyle of peoples, but also their prevailing _________ and _________.

43. Cultural geographers identify a single attribute of a culture as a __________ _________. For example, wearing a ________ is a culture trait in certain societies.

44. A distinct combination of cultural traits is a ________ __________. _________ of cattle is a cultural trait shared by many cultures.

45. A __________ _____________ is an area where cultural traits develop and from which cultural traits diffuse. When such a trait develops in ________ than ______ hearth without being influenced by its development elsewhere, each hearth operates as a case of _________ __________.

46. In 1970, Swedish geographer Torsten Hägerstrand published pioneering research on the role of ______ in __________. Hägerstrand's research revealed how ________, as well as ___________, affects individual human behavior and the dissemination of people and ideas. Sauer and Hägerstrand's fascinating research attracted many geographers to the study of ___________.

47. In combination, time and distance cause ________________ decay in the diffusion process.

48. Not all __________ _________ or innovations diffuse. Prescriptions cultures make about behavior act as __________ ___________ and can pose powerful obstacles to the spread of ideas or innovations.

49. In the case of __________ _____________, an innovation or idea develops in a hearth and remains strong there while also spreading outward.

50. The spread of Under Armour heat gear is a case of ___________ ____________, a pattern in which the main channel of diffusion is some segment of those who are susceptible to (or are already adopting) what is being diffused.

51. The hierarchy of football players, other athletes, and then the __________ _________ among school-age children that followed helps explain the rapid growth of the Under Armour brand, which had revenues of $200 million in 2004 and $2 billion in 2013.

52. Under Armour's performance line prompted __________ _____________ or local experimentation and change in the Nike and Adidas brands. _________ __________, rather than economics, can prohibit contagious diffusion and encourage __________ __________ as well. Not all _______ can be readily and directly adopted by a receiving population; some are simply too _______, too unattainable, too different, or too _____________ for immediate adoption.

53. Relocation diffusion occurs most frequently through __________. ____________ ___________ involves the actual movement of individuals who have already adopted the idea or innovation, and who carry it to a ______ , perhaps distant, locale, where they proceed to disseminate it.

WHAT ARE GEOGRAPHIC CONCEPTS, AND HOW ARE THEY USED IN ANSWERING GEOGRAPHIC QUESTIONS?

54. To think geographically, start by asking a geographic __________, one with a ________ or landscape component. Geographic concepts give us insight and help us understand people, place, space, location, and __________.
55. Huntington and Cushing claim __________ is the critical factor in how humans behave. Each of these theories can be classified as ________ ____________, which holds that human behavior, individually and collectively, is strongly affected by, even controlled or determined by, the physical environment.
56. In response to _______________ _______________, geographers argued that the natural environment merely serves to __________ the range of choices available to a culture. Geographers called this doctrine _____________.
57. Today, much research in human geography focuses on how and why humans have altered their ________________, and on the sustainability of their practices. In the process, the interest in __________ ___________, an area of inquiry concerned with culture as a system of adaptation to and alteration of _____________, has been supplemented by interest in political ecology, an area of inquiry fundamentally concerned with the environmental ___________ of dominant political-economic arrangements and understandings.

Step 4: "Map It" Quiz: Use the maps from the text to answer the questions.

1. Which of the following regions had the highest percentages of undernourished population on the World Hunger map (Figure 1.2)?
   A. North America
   B. South Asia
   C. Latin America
   D. Subsaharan Africa
   E. Southeast Asia

2. Which of the following regions had the highest level of Gross National Income according to the Gross National Income Map (Figure 1.3)?
   A. North America
   B. South Asia
   C. Latin America
   D. Subsaharan Africa
   E. Southeast Asia

3. Which of the following regions had the highest level of arable land according to the map on Farmable (arable) land (Figure 1.4)?
   A. North America
   B. South Asia
   C. Latin America
   D. Subsaharan Africa
   E. Southeast Asia

4. Which of the following regions seems to be the driest on the Average Annual Precipitation of the World map (Figure 1.11)?
   A. North America
   B. Europe
   C. Australia
   D. North Africa and Southwest Asia
   E. Southeast Asia

Step 5: AP-Style Practice Quiz

1. The vast majority of the 1 billion malnourished people on Earth are:
   A. soldiers in countries with insurgencies
   B. people above the age of 65
   C. people with chronic diseases such as HIV/AIDS
   D. women and children
   E. girls under the age of 15

2. Satellite images or aerial photos from a plane are both examples of:
   A. geographic information systems
   B. map generalization
   C. projection
   D. global positioning
   E. remote sensing

3. A region in which the people share one or more cultural traits is a:
   A. functional region
   B. perceptual region
   C. formal region
   D. political region
   E. cultural region

4. A combination of cultural traits is a:
   A. complex culture
   B. cultural hearth
   C. barrier to diffusion
   D. culture region
   E. cultural complex

5. Latitude and longitude will give you the _________ location of a place.
   A. relative
   B. cultural
   C. reference
   D. situation
   E. absolute

6. All geographers, human or physical, are interested in the __________ of a phenomenon.
   A. spatial distribution
   B. absolute location
   C. diffusion
   D. temporal patterns
   E. origin

7. A set of processes that are increasing interactions and interdependence without regard to country borders is:
   A. spatial diffusion
   B. a pandemic
   C. globalization
   D. distance decay
   E. accessibility

8. "From Mannheim Road, go west on North Avenue till you get to 5th Avenue, then north about ¾ of a mile; it's right next to the water tower." This is an example of:
   A. relative location
   B. absolute location
   C. the use of GPS
   D. a mental map
   E. geocaching

9. Why are you not likely to find an all-beef Big Mac at the McDonald's restaurants in India?
   A. Chicken is much cheaper to raise in India.
   B. Most of the people are Hindus who generally do not eat beef.
   C. After the last outbreak of mad cow disease, all the cows were slaughtered.
   D. All the people of India are vegetarians.
   E. Lamb is the preferred red meat in South Asia.

10. The brand Under Armour is an example of which type of diffusion?
    A. relocation
    B. contagious
    C. hierarchical
    D. stimulus
    E. formal

CHAPTER 2:
POPULATION

Name: Sanya Bawa **Period** 8 **Date**______

Chapter Title: Population

Chapter # 2 **Pgs.** 29 **to** 58

The Five Steps to Chapter Success Checklist

Step 1: Read the Chapter Summary below and preview the Key Questions.
Step 2: Complete the Pre-Reading Activity (PRA) for this chapter.
Step 3: Read the chapter and complete the guided worksheet.
Step 4: Take the "Map It!" Quiz.
Step 5: Take an AP-style Practice Quiz.

STEP 1: Chapter Summary, Key Questions, Chapter Outline, and Geographic Concepts

Chapter Summary

In the late 1700s, Thomas Malthus sounded warning bells about the rapidly growing population in Great Britain. He feared a massive famine would soon "check" the growing population, bringing widespread suffering. Although the famine in Great Britain did not take place as he predicted, the rapidly growing worldwide population made many more follow Malthus's trajectory, issuing similar warnings about the population explosion over the last two centuries.

The growth rate of the world population has certainly slowed, but human suffering is not over yet. Dozens of countries still face high death rates and high birth rates. Even in countries where the death rate is low, slowed population growth is often a result of horrid sanitary and medical conditions that lead to high infant and child mortality, diseases such as AIDS that ravage the population and orphan the young, or famines that governments deny and that global organizations cannot ameliorate.

Population pyramids illustrate that as wealthier countries worry about supporting their aging populations, poorer countries have problems of their own. A high birth rate in a poor country does not necessarily mean overpopulation—some of the highest population densities in the world are found in wealthy countries. Even poor countries that have lowered their birth rates and their death rates are constantly negotiating what is morally acceptable to their people and their cultures.

Geography offers much for the study of population. Through geography we can see differences in population problems across space, how what happens at one scale affects what goes on at other scales, and how different cultures and countries approach population questions.

Key Questions

Field Note: Basic Infrastructure	p. 29–30
1. Where in the world do people live and why?	p. 31–36
2. Why do populations rise or fall in particular places?	p. 36–46
3. Why does population composition matter?	p. 46–47
4. How does the geography of health influence population dynamics?	p. 47–56
5. How do governments affect population change?	p. 56-–58

Step 2: Pre-Reading Activity (PRA)

1. Write down the Key Question with the fewest pages and then the most pages.

Key Question	# of Pages
Why does population composition matter?	2
Why do populations rise/fall in particular places?	10

2. After looking over the key questions and reading the chapter summary, write a few sentences about what you expect to learn in general in this chapter.

   Population and examples as to where and why people live in certain places

3. How many world maps are there in this chapter? 10 (Go to Student Companion Website and print out organizers for help.)

4. Read the Field Note introduction of the chapter and list three specific facts you learned.

   -air pollution in china
   -unhealthy Chinese air
   -US department of state measures air pollution

5. Go to Step 1 and look at the Geographic Concepts. Create a list of terms you think you know and terms you need to know.

I THINK I KNOW	I NEED TO LEARN
population	child mortality
migration	morally acceptable
pollution	

Step 3: Chapter 2 Guided Worksheet

Directions: As you read the chapter, fill in the blanks on the guided worksheet.

FIELD NOTE—BASIC INFRASTRUCTURE

1. Shanghai now has the longest metro system on Earth—a system capable of transporting 5 million people a day.
2. China's biggest urban challenge may be water as it already has little to spare. Some 70 percent of water use today traces back to agriculture, but demand from urban consumers and commercial enterprise is on the rise.

WHERE IN THE WORLD DO PEOPLE LIVE AND WHY?

3. Demography is the study of population in general perspective. Population geographers work in tandem with demographers, seeking answers to the problems posed by these variations.
4. Demographers report the population density of a country as a measure of total population relative to land size. No country has an even distributed population, and arithmetic population figures do not reflect the emptiness of most of Alaska and the spareness of population in much of the West.
5. A more insightful index of population density relates the total population of a country or region to the area of arable (farmable) land it contains. This approach yields a physiologic population density figure, which specifies the number of people per unit area of agriculturally productive land
6. People are not distributed evenly across the world or within a country. In addition to studying population densities, geographers study population distributions —the arrangement of people on the Earth's surface. Geographers often represent population distributions using dot maps, with each dot representing a certain number of people.
7. Today, contrasts between crowded countrysides and bustling cities on the one hand and empty areas on the other hand have only intensified. At the global scale, where one dot

on a map represents 100,000 people, 3 major clusters of population jump out. Each of the three largest population clusters is on the Eurasian landmass. The fourth largest is in North America.

8. The most extensive area of dark shading lies in East Asia, primarily in China but also in Korea and Japan. In addition to high population density in China's large cities, ribbons of high population density extend into the interior along the Yangtze and Yellow River valleys.
9. The second major population concentration also lies in Asia and is similar in many ways to that of East Asia. At the heart of this cluster of more than 1.5 billion people lies India. The concentration extends into Pakistan and Bangladesh and onto the island of Sri Lanka.
10. An axis of dense population extends from Ireland and the United Kingdom into Russia and includes large parts of Germany, Poland, Ukraine, and Belarus. It also includes the Netherlands and Belgium, parts of France, and northern Italy. This European cluster contains over 715 million inhabitants, less than half the population of the South Asia cluster.
11. North America has one quite densely populated region, stretching along the urban areas of the East Coast, from Washington, D.C., in the south to Boston, Massachusetts, in the north. Urban geographers use the term megalopolis to refer to such huge urban agglomerations.
12. When the United States planned and conducted its 2010 population census, the government ran advertisements on television and sent mailings encouraging every person in the country to be counted.

WHY DO POPULATIONS RISE OR FALL IN PARTICULAR PLACES?

13. Ehrlich and others warned that the world's population was increasing too quickly—and was outpacing our food production! In his work Malthus warned that the world's population was increasing faster than the food supplies needed to sustain it. His reasoning was that food supplies grew linearly, adding acreage and crops incrementally by year, whereas population grew exponentially, compounding on the year before.
14. Malthus's predictions assumed that food production is confined spatially, that what people can eat within a country depends on what is grown in the country. We now know that assumption does not hold true; countries are not closed systems.
15. One basic demographic indicator is the natural increase of the population in a given place—calculated by subtracting the total number of deaths from the total number of births. Focusing solely on natural increase, however, misses two other key pieces of the demographic picture: immigration, which along with births adds to the total population, and emigration (outmigration), which along with deaths reduces the total population.
16. The world map of population growth rates (Figure 2.7), displayed by country, confirms the wide range of natural increases in different geographic regions. The map also reveals continuing high growth rates in Muslim countries of North Africa and Southwest Asia, including Sudan (2.6 percent), Yemen (2.7 percent), Afghanistan (2.8 percent), and the Palestinian territories (2.9 percent).

17. As Figure 2.7 shows, the Slowest growing countries—including those with declining rates of natural population increase—lie in the economically wealthier areas of the world extending from the United States and Canada across Europe and Japan.
18. Between 1900 and 2000, the world's population rose from 1.6 billion people to 6.1 billion, and in 2011, it reached 7 billion. This growth is not simply a result of women having more children. Instead, the last century of population growth saw greatly expanded life expectancies.
19. Demographers measure whether a population can replace its deaths with births by looking at total fertility rates (TFRs). To reach replacement levels—to keep a population stable over time without immigration—the women of childbearing age in a country need a TFR of 2.1. The TFR reports the average number of children born to a woman of childbearing age.
20. The impact of the aging population of Europe can be seen in its old-age dependency ratio, which reports the relationship between the number of people over the age of 65 and the working-age population between 15 and 64. An aging population requires substantial social adjustments. Older people retire and eventually suffer ________ problems, so they need pensions and medical care.
21. One way to explain the growth rate in world population is to compare the population's rate of growth to its doubling time.
22. As a result of falling TFRs in both the developing and developed world, demographers no longer caution about doubling time. With women having fewer children, many demographers are predicting the world may reach maximum population growth in the next 50 years.
23. In the 1950s, India became the first country in the world to institute a population planning program, before the fear of worldwide overpopulation and a global population bomb spread.
24. Today, most Indian State governments are using advertising and persuasion to encourage families to have fewer children.
25. Demographers have used data on baptisms and funerals from churches in Great Britain to study changes in birth and death rates of the population. They calculated the crude birth rate (CBR)—the number of live births per year per thousand people in the population—and the crude death rate (CDR)—the number of deaths per year per thousand people. Demographers call the shift in population growth the demographic transition.

WHY DOES POPULATION COMPOSITION MATTER?

26. Maps showing the regional distribution and density of populations tell us about the number of people in countries or regions, but they cannot reveal other aspects of those populations: the number of men and women and their ages. These aspects of population, the population composition, are important because a populous country in which half the population is very young has quite different problems from a populous country in which a large proportion of the population is elderly.
27. Age and sex are key indicators of population composition, and demographers and geographers use population pyramids to represent these traits visually. Population

pyramids are used to display the percentages of each age group in a total population (normally five -year increments) by a horizontal bar whose length represents its share. Males in the group are to the left of the center line, females to the right.

28. In poorer countries, where birth and death rates generally remain high, the pyramid looks like an evergreen tree, with wide branches at the base and short ones near the top. Wealthy countries have population pyramids that do not look like pyramids at all. Families become smaller, children fewer. The "pyramid" looks like a slightly lopsided vase, with the largest components of the population not at the bottom but in the middle.

HOW DOES THE GEOGRAPHY OF HEALTH INFLUENCE POPULATION DYNAMICS?

29. One of the leading measures of the condition of a country's population is the infant mortality rate. It is recorded as a baby's death during the first year. Infant and child mortality reflect the overall health of a society.
30. The lowest infant mortality rate among larger populations has long been reported by Japan, with 2.2 deaths per 1000 live births in a country of over 127 million people.
31. The IMR in the United States also varies by region, with the highest IMR in the _______ and the lowest in the Northeast (Figure 2.19). Race, ethnicity, social class, education levels, and access to health care also vary by region in the United States; these correlations are found for many health problems ranging from diabetes to heart disease.
32. Infants who survive their first year of life still do not have a long life expectancy in the poorer areas of the world. The child mortality rate, which records the deaths of children between the ages of 1 and 5, remains staggeringly high in much of Africa and Asia, notably in the protein-deficient tropical and subtropical zones. In some countries, more than one in five children still ____ between their first and fifth birthdays, a terrible record in the twenty-first century.
33. Yet another indicator of a society's well-being lies in the life expectancy of its members at birth, that is, the number of years, on average, someone may expect to remain alive. Life expectancies can change in relatively short order. For example, in South Africa, one of the countries hardest hit by the ______ epidemic, the life expectancy rose from 56.6 to 60 years between 2009 and 2011 as a result of treatment and education programs.
34. As we have seen, health is fundamentally influenced by local sanitation conditions. The availability of clean water plays a particularly critical role. Human-driven environmental pollution is also a factor; polluted water and air, and degraded lands, undermine health and well-being. Disease also has a great impact on human health.
35. Some 65 percent of all diseases are known as infectious diseases, resulting from an invasion of parasites and their multiplication in the body. Malaria is an infectious disease. The remainder can be divided into the chronic or degenerate diseases, the maladies of longevity and old age such as heart disease, and the genetic or inherited diseases we can trace to our ancestry, that is, the chromosomes and genes that define our makeup. Sickle-cell anemia, hemophilia, and lactose intolerance are among these genetic diseases.

36. A disease is endemic when it prevails over a small area. A disease is epidemic when it spreads over a large region. A pandemic disease is global in scope.

37. Infectious diseases continue to sicken and kill millions of people annually. Malaria, an old tropical disease, alone still takes more than a million lives annually and infects about 300 million people today.

38. A vectured infectious disease such as malaria is transmitted by an intermediary vector—in malaria's case a mosquito. Nonvectured infectious diseases are transmitted by direct contact between host and victim. A kiss, a handshake, or even contact with someone's breath can transmit influenza, a cold, or some other familiar malady.

39. Malaria is an infectious disease spread by mosquitoes that carry the parasite in their saliva. Malaria occurs throughout the world, except in higher latitudes and altitudes and drier environments.

40. Low life expectancies in some parts of the world are caused by the ravages of HIV—a disease identified in Africa in the early 1980s. Medical geographers estimate that in 1980 about 200,000 people were infected with HIV (Human Immunodeficiency Virus, which causes AIDS), all of them Africans. By 2012, the number worldwide exceeded 75 million, according to the United Nations AIDS Program, with 10 percent (25 million) of all cases in sub-saharan Africa! The infection rate worldwide has decreased 33 percent since 2001 and is continuing to slow, but eastern Europe and Central Asia have recently seen a surge in HIV infection.

41. Chronic diseases (also called degenerative diseases) are the afflictions of middle and old age, reflecting higher life expectancies. Among the chronic diseases, heart disease, cancers, and strokes rank as the leading diseases in this category, but pneumonia, diabetes, and liver diseases also take their toll. At the global scale, infectious diseases such as tuberculosis and pneumonia are less serious threats than they once were, but cancer and heart disease take a high toll.

42. Humans are constantly altering Earth's surface in ways that have the potential to influence health and the spread of diseases. There is growing evidence, for example, that climate-change-induced increases in precipitation and flooding, along with rising temperatures, are expanding the geographic reach of diseases that are transmitted by mosquitoes. Addressing this problem requires geographic studies that look at the impacts of ecosystem changes on health issues in particular places.

HOW DO GOVERNMENTS AFFECT POPULATION CHANGE?

43. Over the past century, many of the world's governments have instituted policies designed to influence the overall growth rate or ethnic ratios within the population. These policies fall into three groups: expansive, eugenic, restrictive.

44. In the past, some governments engaged in eugenic population policies, which were designed to favor one racial or cultural sector of the population over others. Germany was a drastic case in point, but other countries also have pursued eugenic strategies, though in more subtle ways.

45. Today many of the world's governments seek to reduce the rate of natural increase through various forms of restrictive population policies. These policies range from toleration of officially unapproved means of birth control to outright prohibition of

large families. China's one child policy, instituted after the end of the maust period in the 1970s, drastically reduced China's growth rate from one of the world's fastest to one of the world's slowest.

46. In Sweden, couples that work and have small children receive cash payments, tax incentives, job leaves, and work flexibility that last up to 1.5 years after the birth of a child. When the Swedish population slowed shortly thereafter, however, so did the birth rate.
47. Some areas of the world with low population growth rates are in the very heart of the Roman Catholic world. Roman Catholic doctrine opposes birth control and abortion.
48. Among Islamic countries, the geographic pattern is the opposite. Saudi Arabia, home to Mecca—the hearth of Islam—has a relatively high population growth rate, with the population increasing at 1.8 percent each year. But in Indonesia, thousands of miles from Mecca, the government began a nationwide family planning program in 1970 when the population growth rate was 2.6 percent.

Step 4: "Map It!" Quiz: Use the maps from the text to answer the questions.

1. Which of the following regions has the fewest number of dots based on the World Population Distribution map (Figure 2.5)?
   A. North America
   B. Europe
   C. South Asia
   D. Subsaharan Africa
   E. Australia

2. The general pattern of the most dense locations appears to be __________, based on the World Population Density Map (Figure 2.6).
   A. the Southern Hemisphere
   B. the Western Hemisphere
   C. polar regions
   D. coastal areas
   E. arid regions

3. Which of the following regions is experiencing the highest population growth based on the World Population Growth Map (Figure 2.7)?
   A. North Africa and Southwest Asia
   B. Subsaharan Africa
   C. South America
   D. South Asia
   E. East Asia

4. Which of the following countries experienced a drop of fertility below replacement level in or after 1989 according to the Fertility Map (Figure 2.8)?
   A. China
   B. the United States
   C. France
   D. Mexico
   E. India

5. Which region has the highest crude birth rate based on the Crude Birth Rate Map (Figure 2.13)?
   A. Latin America
   B. North America
   C. North Africa and Southwest Asia
   D. South Asia
   E. Subsaharan Africa

6. Looking at the map on mortality, one finds that China, India, and Mexico's mortality is lower than that in the United States. Which of the following is the best reason (Figure 2.18)?
   A. better available medicine and hospitals outside of the United States
   B. warmer climate outside of the United States
   C. larger populations mean more workers outside of the United States
   D. younger populations outside of the United States
   E. fewer infectious diseases outside of the United States

7. Which of the following regions has the lowest infant mortality rates (Figure 2.18)?
   A. Latin America
   B. Europe
   C. South Asia
   D. Southeast Asia
   E. East Asia

8. After looking at the Mothers Index map, which of the following statements is true about the location of more developed countries (Figure 2.20)?
   A. more in the Western Hemisphere than Eastern Hemisphere
   B. more in the Southern Hemisphere than the Northern Hemisphere
   C. clustered at the Equator
   D. more in the Northern Hemisphere than the Southern Hemisphere
   E. more on island nations

9. Where is life expectancy at birth the highest according to the Life Expectancy Map (Figure 2.21)?
   A. South Asia
   B. East Asia
   C. Southeast Asia
   D. Europe
   E. North America

10. According to the Malaria Endemicity Map, where do outbreaks remain high (Figure 2.22)?
    A. near the equator
    B. polar regions
    C. Western Hemisphere only
    D. Eastern Hemisphere only
    E. China

Step 5: AP-Style Practice Quiz

1. All of the following are components of population growth EXCEPT:
    A. crude birth rate
    B. crude death rate
    C. immigration
    D. density
    E. emigration

2. An index that relates a country's population density to its available arable land is known as:
    A. physiologic density
    B. population density
    C. arithmetic density
    D. distribution density
    E. crop density

3. The region of the world with the highest population is:
    A. Southeast Asia
    B. Europe
    C. North America
    D. South America
    E. East Asia

4. According to the text, the world's population in 2011 was:
    A. 7 million
    B. 10 billion
    C. 9 million
    D. 7 billion
    E. 15 billion

5. Which of the following statements is true?
    A. The slowest growing countries are in the economic core.
    B. The slowest growing countries are in the economic periphery.
    C. The fastest growing countries are in southern Africa.
    D. Russia's population is in decline because of its one-child policy.
    E. China's family planning programs once included guns exchanged for sterilization.

6. In what two stages of the demographic transition model does population grow rapidly?
   A. stages 1 and 2
   B. stages 2 and 3
   C. stages 3 and 4
   D. stages 1 and 4
   E. stages 4 and 5

7. All of the following are directly indicated on a population pyramid EXCEPT:
   A. percentage of population
   B. life expectancy
   C. age cohorts in five-year increments
   D. males
   E. females

8. Which of the following countries has the highest life expectancies in the world?
   A. the United States
   B. Canada
   C. Sweden
   D. France
   E. Japan

9. Where in the world has the AIDS epidemic had the greatest impact?
   A. inner-city United States
   B. Russia
   C. Subsaharan Africa
   D. Southeast Asia
   E. Southwest China

10. In countries where cultural traditions restrict educational and professional opportunities for women, and men dominate as a matter of custom, what is the usual impact on population growth rates?
    A. rates of natural increase tend to be high.
    B. rates of natural increase tend to be low.
    C. total fertility rates tend to be low.
    D. infant mortality tends to be low.
    E. there is no discernible correlation.

CHAPTER 3: MIGRATION

The Five Steps to Chapter Success

Step 1: Read the Chapter Summary below and preview the Key Questions.
Step 2: Complete the Pre-Reading Activity (PRA) for this chapter.
Step 3: Read the chapter and complete the guided worksheet.
Step 4: Review all the World maps and take the "Map It!" quiz
Step 5: Take an AP-style Practice Quiz.

STEP 1: Chapter Summary and Key Questions

Chapter Summary

In the last 500 years, humans have traveled the globe, mapped it, connected it through globalization, and migrated across it. In this chapter, we discussed major global, regional, and national migration flows. Migration can occur as a result of a conscious decision, resulting in a voluntary migration flow, or migration can occur under duress, resulting in forced migration. Both kinds of migration have left an indelible mark on the world and on its cultural landscapes. Governments attempt to strike a balance among the need for migrant labor, the desire to help people in desperate circumstances, and the desire to stem the tide of migration.

As the world's population mushrooms, the volume of migrants will expand. In an increasingly open and interconnected world, neither physical barriers nor politically motivated legislation will stem tides that are as old as human history. Migrations will also further complicate an already complex global cultural pattern—raising questions about identity, race, ethnicity, language, and religion, the topics we turn to in the next three chapters.

Key Questions

Field Note: Risking Lives for Remittances	p. 60–63
1. What is migration?	p. 63–66
2. Why do people migrate?	p. 66–73
3. Where do people migrate?	p. 73–86
4. How do governments affect migration?	p. 86–88

Step 2: Pre-Reading Activity (PRA)

1. Write down the Key Question with the fewest pages and then the most pages.

Key Question	# of Pages
How do governments affect migration?	3
Where do people migrate?	14

2. After looking over the key questions and reading the chapter summary, write a few sentences about what you expect to learn in general in this chapter.

Overall, I expect to learn the different migrational patterns of groups with different ethnicities, races and religions.

3. How many world maps are there in this chapter? 2 (Go to Student Companion Website and print out organizers for help.)

4. Read the Field Note introduction of the chapter and list three specific facts you learned.

• US allows unskilled workers into country to fill jobs that Americans don't want
• 13% → 50% of population in cities
• population increase in India causing housing shortage

5. Go to the end of the chapter and look at the Geographic Concepts. Create a list of terms you think you know and terms you need to know.

I THINK I KNOW	I NEED TO LEARN
refugees	distance decay
immigration	genocide
push-pull	cyclic movement
deportation	residential relocation

Step 3: Chapter 3 Guided Worksheet

Directions: As you read the chapter, fill in the blanks on the guided worksheet.

FIELD NOTE– EXPANDING SLUMS

1. More than 60 percent of the people in Mumbai live in slums or shanties like the one shown in Figure 3.1. By 2011, the population in the city more than doubled to 12.5 million, and the larger urban area has a population of more than 20 million.
2. Starting in the 1970s, Indians left rural areas and migrated to urban areas in large numbers because in rural areas landholdings are often too small to support growing families and employment opportunities outside the agricultural sector are cities offer at least the possibility of improved job prospects and a better life.
3. At the global scale, rural-urban migration represents one of the most dramatic shifts in the human geography of the planet over the last century. In 1900, only 13 percent of the world's people lived in cities; now the figure exceeds 50 percent, and it is on the rise.
4. The "Lost Boys of Sudan" fled their homelands between the ages of 7 and 17 in the face of a devastating civil war in the closing decades of the twentieth century. They walked tremendous distances seeking refuge from the conflict. Many ______ their lives along the way; others ended up in refugee camps in Kenya, Uganda, and the more stable parts of Sudan.
5. Monies migrants send home are called remittance. Haitians living in the United States, Canada, and the Caribbean sent home over $1.9 billion in remittances in 2012, a figure equivalent to 30 percent of Haiti's gross domestic product and far outpacing the value of Haitian exports.
6. Not all immigrants are undocumented. Of the estimated 41.7 million immigrants in the United States today, 30 million are documented immigrants.

WHAT IS MIGRATION?

7. Geographers recognize 3 basic types of movement. cyclic movement involves shorter, regular trips away from home for defined amounts of time. Periodic movement involves longer periods away from home undertaken from time to time. Actual migration carries with it a degree of permanence that is not characteristic of the other two forms of movement: The mover may never return "home."
8. Cyclic movement describes a regular journey that begins at a home base and returns to the exact same place. The great majority of people have a periodic movement that takes them through a regular sequence of short moves within a local area. These moves create what geographers call cyclic movement.
9. Commuting is also a cyclic movement. Commuting—the journey from home to work and home again—takes from minutes to hours and can involve several modes of transportation.

10. In Washington, D.C., commuters combine use of their cars, commuter trains, and the metro to travel upwards of 1000 miles a way, each day, commuting not only from the surrounding suburbs but also from Delaware, West Virginia, and central Virginia.
11. Another type of cyclic movement, nomadism, is a matter of survival, culture, and tradition. Nomadism is dwindling across the world, but it can still be found in parts of Asia and Africa.
12. ________ __________ involves a ________ period of time away from the home base than cyclic movement.
13. A specialized form of periodic movement is seasonal, which is a system of pastoral farming in which ranchers move __________ according to the seasonal availability of pastures. This is a periodic form of movement because, unlike classic nomadism, it involves a __________ period of residential relocation in a different place.
14. When movement results in significant relocation across significant distances, it is classified as migration. The process of migration involves the ___________ relocation of an individual, a household, or larger group to a new locale outside the community of origin. International migration, movement ________ country borders, is also called transnational migration.
15. Countries also experience ________ migration—migration that occurs within a ______ country's borders. Early in the twentieth century, a major migration stream took tens of thousands of ________ _________ families from the South of the United States to the industrializing cities of the ________ and Midwest. More recently, __________ opportunities in the ________ have begun to reverse the Great Migration.

WHY DO PEOPLE MIGRATE?

16. Migration can be the result of a _________ _________, a conscious decision to move from one place to the next. It can also be the result of an involuntary action, a ________ __________ imposed on a group of people.
17. ________ __________ involves the imposition of authority or power, producing involuntary movements that cannot be understood based on theories of choice. Voluntary migration occurs after a migrant weighs ________ and _________, even if somewhat desperately or not so rationally.
18. The distinction between forced and voluntary migration is not always ___________. The enormous European migration to the United States during the nineteenth and early twentieth centuries is often cited as a prime example of _________ migration. However, some European migration can be construed as __________.
19. Studies of gender and migration find that, in many regions, ______ are more mobile than women and men migrate _________ than women. Generally, men have more choices of employment than women, and ________ earn ______ than men in the jobs they find at the destination locations.
20. The largest and most devastating forced migration in the history of humanity was the __________ ________ ________ during the European colonial period, which carried tens of millions of Africans from their homes to South America, the Caribbean, and North America.

21. _______ ___________ still happens today. It continues to occur, for example, in the form of countermigration, in which governments ________ migrants who enter or attempt to enter their countries illegally and return the migrants to their home countries. _______ ___________ is another ongoing example of forced migration and an issue of concern in the _______________ community.

22. Over a century ago, British demographer Ernst __________ sought an answer to the question of why people voluntarily migrate. He studied internal migration in England, and on the basis of his data he proposed several laws of __________, many of which are still relevant today, including:

    1. Every migration flow generates a return or _______________.
    2. The majority of migrants move a _______ distance.
    3. Migrants who move longer distances tend to choose __________ destinations.
    4. _________ residents are _______ migratory than inhabitants of rural areas.
    5. ____________ are less likely to make international moves than young adults.

23. Ravenstein's idea is an early observation of the _______ ________, which predicts interaction between places on the basis of their _________ size and _________between them.

24. When an individual, family, or group of people makes a _________decision to migrate, push and pull factors come into play. ______ factors are the conditions and perceptions that help the migrant decide to ________ a place. _______ factors are the circumstances that effectively _________ the migrant to certain locales from other places, the decision of where to go.

25. When considering pull factors, the principle of ___________ comes into play. Prospective migrants are likely to have more ________ perceptions of _______ places than of farther ones, which confirms the notion that the intensity of human activity, process, or function _________ as distance from its source increases.

26. Migration streams may appear on maps as long, unbroken routes, but in fact they often consist of a series of _________, a phenomenon known as ______ migration.

27. Research has shown that typically a ____________ of factors, not just one, leads to deciding it is time to move and deciding where to go.

28. Each __country__ around the world determines who is allowed to __leave__ and under what circumstances. Undocumented migrants choose quite __sneaky__ options for finding their way into the country than documented migrants do because they do not want to be caught for fear of ____________, being sent back home.

29. __________ has driven countless millions from their homelands and continues to do so. Gender, ethnicity, race, and ________ are all factors in the decision to migrate. ________ relationships already embedded in society enable the flow of migrants around the world.

30. Throughout history, ___________ regimes have engendered migration streams. Desperate migrants fled _________ and Cambodia by the hundreds of thousands as new regimes came to power in the wake of the _________ War.

31. The dreadful conflict that engulfed the former ____________ during the 1990s drove as many as 3 million people from their homes, mostly into western Europe. Natural crises, including earthquakes, hurricanes, volcanic eruptions, and tsunamis, also stimulate movement. Because many migrants escape, the net outflow generated by such momentary crises is often large, but this is not always the case.
32. People who fear that their culture and traditions will not survive a major ____________ ____________, and who are able to migrate to places they perceive as cultural, will often do so.
33. For some migrants, emigration is no longer the problematic and hazardous journey it used to be. Although most migrants, especially nomads, still move by foot, some use modern forms of transportation and technology, the availability of which can itself encourage migration. Advances in communication technology strengthen the role of core countries as push or pull factors.
34. When a migrant chooses a destination and emails, calls, or communicates through others to tell family and friends at home about the new place, the migrant helps create a positive perception of the country for family and friends, and may promise help with migration by providing housing and assistance obtaining a job. Geographers call flows along and through kinship links chain migration.

WHERE DO PEOPLE MIGRATE?

35. Before 1500, long-distance migration occurred haphazardly, typically in pursuit of spices, fame, or exploration. Things changed in the age of European colonization. Colonization is a physical process whereby the colonizing entity takes over another place, putting its own government in charge and either moving its own people into the place or bringing in indentured outsiders to gain control of the people and the land.
36. The major flows of global migration from 1500 on are shown in Figure 3.10. The migration flows include movements from Europe to North America (1); from southern Europe to South and Central America (2); from Britain and Ireland to Africa and Australia (3); from Africa to the Americas during the period of slavery (4); and from India to eastern Africa, Southeast Asia, and Caribbean America (5). Among the greatest human migrations in recent centuries was the flow from Europe to the Americas.
37. Western European governments called the labor migrants guest workers—a term that is now used to describe migrant labor in other places as well.
38. A significant recent example of regional migration is the movement of peoples from Mexico and countries farther south into the United States.
39. Regional migration flows also center on reconnecting cultural groups across borders. A migration stream with enormous consequences is the flow of Jewish immigrants to Israel. Through a series of wars, Israel expanded its area of territorial control (Figure 3.13) and actively built settlements for new Jewish immigrants in Palestinian territories (Figure 3.14). Jewish immigrants from the Eurasian region continue to migrate to Israel.
40. National migration flows can also be thought of as internal migration flows. Internal migration can be quite significant. In the United States, a massive two-centuries-long migration stream has carried the center of population west and more recently also south, as Figure 3.15 shows.

41. Russia also experienced a major internal migration, but in Russia people migrated east, from the heartland of the Russian state (near Moscow and St. Petersburg) to the shores of the Pacific. During the communist period, the Soviet government also employed a policy of Russification, which sought to assimilate all the people in the Soviet territory into the Russian culture.
42. The vast majority of refugees do not make it far from home. The Office of the United Nations High Commissioner for Refugees (UNHCR) estimates that 83 percent of refugees flee to a country in the same region as their home country.
43. The 1951 Refugee Convention defines a refugee as "a person who has a well-founded fear of being persecuted for reasons of race, religion, nationality, membership of a particular social group, or political opinion."
44. Perhaps the biggest problem with the UN definition has to do with internally displaced persons (called IDPs, sometimes called internal refugees). Internally displaced persons are people who have been displaced within their own regions, such as the victims of Hurricane Katrina, but they do not cross international borders as they flee. IDPs tend to remain undercounted, if not almost invisible.
45. In the 1990s, hostilities broke out between the Hutu and Tutsi ethnic groups in Rwanda that led to a genocide, killing hundreds of thousands and a disastrous exodus of more than one million refugees who fled to neighboring Democratic Republic of the Congo (then called Zaire), Tanzania, and Uganda.
46. The Gulf War of 1991 and the Iraq War of 2003 have generated millions of refugees in the region. Following the outbreak of civil war in Syria in 2011, hundreds of thousands of Kurds, some of whom had sought refuge in Syria only a few years earlier, were forced to flee.
47. In 1996, the Taliban, an Islamic fundamentalist movement that began in northwest Pakistan, emerged in Afghanistan and took control of most of the country, imposing strict Islamic rule and suppressing the factional conflicts that had prevailed since the Soviet withdrawal.
48. In 2004, U.S. Secretary of State Colin Powell labeled the Janjaweed's actions in Darfur a genocide. The 1948 Convention on Genocide defines genocide as "acts committed with intent to destroy, in whole or in part, a national, ethnical, racial, or religious group."
49. The other major refugee problem in South Asia stems from a civil war in Sri Lanka. This conflict, which formally ended in 2009, arose from demands by minority Tamils for an independent state on the Sinhalese-dominated and -controlled island.
50. In the 1990s, the collapse of Yugoslavia and its associated conflicts created the largest refugee crisis in Europe since the end of World War II.

HOW DO GOVERNMENTS AFFECT MIGRATION?

51. The control of immigration, legal and illegal, the granting of asylum to asylum-seeking refugees, and the fate of cross-border refugees, permanent and temporary, have become hot issues around the world.

52. In the United States, restrictive legislation on immigration can be traced to 1882, when Congress approved the Oriental Exclusion Acts (1882–1907). Congress designed immigration laws to prevent the immigration of Chinese people to California.
53. Changes in a country's migration policies are reflected in the number of people entering the country and the origin of the immigrants (see Figure 3.21).
54. Many countries practice selective immigration, in which individuals with certain backgrounds (criminal records, poor health, subversive activities) are barred from entering. Other countries have specific requirements.
55. Since September 11, 2001, U.S. government immigration policies have incorporated security concerns. After September 11, the U.S. government designated 33 countries as places where al-Qaeda or other terrorist groups operate, and the government automatically detained anyone from one of these 33 countries who entered the United States looking for asylum under a policy called "Operation Liberty Shield."

Step 4: "Map It!" Quiz: Use the maps from the text to answer the questions.

1. According to the Human Migration in Modern Times map, why are people of Indian descent found in South Africa (Figure 3.10)?
   A. They were the original inhabitants.
   B. They were volunteer migrants from North America.
   C. They were volunteer migrants from India.
   D. They were forced migrants from North America.
   E. They were forced migrants from India.

2. According the Average Refugees by Origin Map, which two countries had the largest number of refugees (Figure 3.16)?
   A. China and Vietnam
   B. Colombia and Russia
   C. Somalia and Sudan
   D. Iraq and Afghanistan
   E. Indonesia and India

Step 5: AP-Style Practice Quiz

1. What is the name for the seasonal migration of farmers and their cattle up and down the mountain slopes of Switzerland?
   A. internal migration
   B. commuting
   C. activity spaces
   D. transhumance
   E. voluntary migration

2. In mathematical terms, it is the multiplication of the populations of two places divided by the distance between them.
   A. law of migration
   B. intervening opportunity
   C. push-pull equation
   D. transhumance
   E. gravity model

3. Which of the following describes the term for a Haitian working in the United States and sending money back home to his/her family?
   A. the gravity model
   B. push factor
   C. immigration
   D. remittances
   E. the Bracero program

4. Which of the following is an example of chain migration?
   A. Drought leads to famine in the Punjab, which leads to desperation, which leads to Emigration.
   B. The Dutch first brought people from Indonesia to the Caribbean, and then from other Dutch colonies around the world.
   C. One village after another comes under attack by rebels, forcing the people of those villages to migrate to safer areas.
   D. In a rural town in Jalisco, Mexico, one person manages to migrate legally to the United States and settles in Elgin, Illinois. He finds a job and prospers, and writes home of his success. Ten years later there is a community of 350 people from Jalisco living in Elgin.
   E. Refers specifically to migrations from Central America, starting in Mexico, then moving through the Central American states of Guatemala, Belize, Honduras, Nicaragua, El Salvador, Costa Rica, and finally Panama.

5. Which of the following was NOT given as a reason for the disparity between the UN's calculation of global refugees and the numbers given by other organizations?
   A. The UN inflates the numbers, thus requiring a bigger budget to provide aid to refugees.
   B. There are different definitions for what constitutes a refugee.
   C. Refugees often flee to remote areas where they cannot be counted.
   D. Governments sometimes manipulate refugee numbers for political reasons.
   E. A distinction is made between internally displaced persons and international refugees.

6. Which of the following is a consequence of the large number of men who died in both world wars?
   A. Large numbers of Algerians migrated to German-speaking countries.
   B. After the war, women replaced men in factory jobs.
   C. Germany, in particular, brought in guest workers, mainly from Turkey.
   D. Most European countries adopted restrictive immigration policies.
   E. The center of European population shifted to the southeast.

7. What is one of the consequences of the fences the United States built along the border with Mexico, especially those separating cities on both sides of the border?
   A. Since the fences are designed to be attractive and friendly, relations between the countries have improved.
   B. U.S. companies are investing in more maquiladoras.
   C. Desperate migrants have started carrying guns and confronting the border patrol.
   D. Remittances from the United States to Mexico have been sharply reduced.
   E. It forces illegal immigrants to cross in hostile terrain, such as deserts, leading to more people dying.

8. The practice of barring certain individuals (those with criminal records, poor health, subversive activities) from coming into the country is known as:
   A. selective immigration
   B. internal migration
   C. quota system
   D. forced migration
   E. chain migration

9. Your daily routines describe which type of movement?
   A. cyclic
   B. periodic
   C. transhumance
   D. internal migration
   E. nomadism

10. Which two ethnic groups immigrated to the United States in the greatest numbers since the 1990s?
    A. Europeans and Asians
    B. Latinos and Asians
    C. Africans and Europeans
    D. Australians and Asians
    E. Latinos and Australia

CHAPTER 4:

LOCAL CULTURE, POPULAR CULTURE, AND CULTURAL LANDSCAPES

Name: ______________________________ **Period** __________ **Date** __________

Chapter Title: ____

Chapter # ______________________________ **Pgs.** __________ **to** __________

The Five Steps to Chapter Success

Step 1: Read the Chapter Summary below and preview the Key Questions.
Step 2: Complete the Pre-Reading Activity (PRA) for this chapter.
Step 3: Read the chapter and complete the guided worksheet.
Step 4: Read the maps and take the "Map It!"quiz
Step 5: Take an AP-style Practice Quiz

STEP 1: Chapter Summary and Key Questions

Chapter Summary

Advances in transportation and communications technology help popular culture diffuse at record speeds around the world today. Popular culture changes quickly, offering new music, foods, fashions, and sports. Popular culture envelopes and infiltrates local cultures, presenting constant challenges to members of local cultures. Some members of local cultures have accepted popular culture, others have rejected it, and still others have forged a balance between the two.

Customs from local cultures are often commodified, propelling them into popular culture. The search for an "authentic" local culture custom generally ends up promoting a stereotyped local culture or glorifying a single aspect of that local culture. Local culture, like popular culture, is dynamic, and the pursuit of authenticity disregards the complexity and fluidity of cultures.

Key Questions

Field Note: Preserving Culture	p. 90–91
1. What are local and popular cultures?	p. 91–93
2. How are local cultures sustained?	p. 93–101
3. How is popular culture diffused?	p. 102–115

Step 2: Pre-Reading Activity (PRA)

1. Write down each of the Key Questions with the fewest pages and then the most pages.

Key Question	# of Pages

2. After looking over the Key Questions and the Chapter Summary write a few sentences about what you expect to learn in general in this chapter.

3. How many world maps are there in this chapter? _____ (Go to Student Companion Website and print out organizers for help.)

4. Read the Field Note introduction of the chapter and list three specific facts you learned.

____
____
____
____
____
____
____

5. Go to Step 1 and look at the Geographic Concepts. Create a list of terms you think you know and terms you need to know.

I THINK I KNOW	I NEED TO LEARN

Step 3: Chapter 4 Guided Worksheet

FIELD NOTE- PRESERVING CULTURES

1. This used to be an __________ restaurant. "Not anymore," the young man with a thick New York accent said to me, offering a few expletives to describe the __________ moving into the neighborhood, as well as a prediction: "It's probably gonna be a Chinese restaurant ______.
2. The United States ___________ constraints on Chinese immigration in 1965, and after that Chinese immigrants moved into _________ in droves. Chinatown expanded into ______ _______, and today only ____ blocks on Mulberry Street constitute the heart of Little Italy.
3. Immigrant groups establish ___________ ___________ in cities, imprinting the place with cultural ________ from their homeland, from eateries to specialty shops to churches. Having a place where people with a __________ _________ belong helps sustain a local culture.

WHAT ARE LOCAL AND POPULAR CULTURES?

4. A _________ is a group of belief systems, norms, and values practiced by a people. Although this definition of culture sounds simple, the concept of culture is actually quite ________.
5. The idea is that a _______ _________ is small, incorporates a homogeneous population, is typically rural, and is cohesive in cultural traits, whereas ________ _________ is large, incorporates heterogeneous populations, is typically urban, and experiences quickly changing cultural traits.
6. A _________ _________ is a group of people in a particular place who see themselves as a collective or a _________, who share experiences, customs, and traits, and who work to ________ those traits and customs in order to claim uniqueness and to distinguish themselves from others.
7. The _________ _________ of a group of people includes things they construct, such as art, houses, clothing, sports, dance, and foods. ______________ ________ includes beliefs, practices, aesthetics (what is seen as attractive), and values of a group of people. What members of a local culture produce in their material culture reflects the _______ and _______ of their nonmaterial culture.
8. In popular culture, _________ trends spread very quickly through the interconnected world; it is a classic case of ____________ diffusion. Hierarchical diffusion can occur through a __________ of places.
9. The hierarchy in the fashion world typically begins with the runways of major fashion houses in world ________, including London, Milan, Paris, and New York, which act as the _________, the point of origin.

HOW ARE LOCAL CULTURES SUSTAINED?

10. During the 1800s and into the 1900s, the U.S. government had an official policy of _____________. Today, several churches and governments have ____________ for assimilation policies.

11. Local cultures are sustained through __________. A custom is a ___________ that a group of people routinely follows. People have customs regarding _____ parts of their ________, from eating and drinking to dancing and sports. To sustain a local culture, the people must retain their __________.
12. A local culture can also work to avoid _________ _____________, the process by which other cultures adopt customs and knowledge and use them for their own benefit. Around the world, local cultures desire to keep popular culture _____, keep their culture intact, and maintain control over customs and knowledge.
13. Members of local cultures in _______ areas often have an easier time maintaining their cultures because of their isolation. By living together in a rural area, members of a local culture can more easily keep external influences on the _________.
14. Unlike the Amish, _____________ readily accept technologies that help them in their agricultural pursuits.
15. In the late 1990s, the Makah American Indians of Neah Bay, Washington, did what environmentalists considered unthinkable: They reinstated the ________ hunt.
16. The __________ wanted to hunt with their traditional canoes and harpoons because they wanted to hunt as the tribe's elders and ancestors did. The International Whaling Commission dictated that the Makah hunt gray whales with a .50 caliber ________, arguing the rifle would kill the whale more quickly and humanely than the harpoons their ancestors used.
17. The residents of Lindsborg, Kansas, proclaim their town _______ _________, U.S.A. Geographer Steven Schnell asked why a town of 3300, which a few decades ago had little or no sign of Swedishness on its landscape, transformed itself into a place where _________ culture is celebrated every day in gift stores on Main Street and in buffets in restaurants.
18. Geographer James Shortridge (1996) refers to this as ______________, seeking out the regional culture and reinvigorating it in response to the uncertainty of the modern world.
19. Some local cultures have successfully built a world apart, a place to practice their customs, within a major city by constructing tight-knit _______ ___________.
20. The process through which something (a name, a ________, an idea, or even a person) that previously was not regarded as an object to be bought or sold ____________ an object that can be bought, sold, and traded in the world market is called ______________.
21. When commodification occurs, the question of __________ follows. When local cultures or customs are __________, usually one image or experience is typecast as the "authentic" image or experience of that culture, and it is that image or experience that the ________ or buyer desires.
22. The act of ___________ commodifying the mystique of local cultures to drive profits can, however, be less obvious to the consumer. The ___________ Brewing Company of Dublin, Ireland, created a business plan in 1991 aimed at capitalizing on the global mystique of the traditional Irish pub. Guinness saw the sales of its stout beer declining in Ireland and the United Kingdom and decided to go __________.

HOW IS POPULAR CULTURE DIFFUSED?

23. During the twentieth century, however, the pace of diffusion ________ to months, weeks, days, and in some cases even hours.
24. The map of Facebook users highlights the __________________ of individuals around the world, and it also points out the lack of interconnection between individuals in _______ with the rest of the world via this social media tool.
25. Transportation and communication technologies have altered __________ _______. No longer does a map with a bull's eye surrounding the hearth of an innovation describe how ________ the innovation will diffuse to areas around it. Rather, what geographer David Harvey called ____________ __________________ explains how quickly innovations diffuse and refers to how interlinked two places are through transportation and communication technologies
26. Like new music or other forms of popular culture, extreme sports have become more _____________, mainstream, and __________________.
27. Identity and the desire to remain outside of popular culture will continue to spur the creation of_________ ___________ to rival the big three.
28. Geographers realize that ________ cultures will interpret, choose, and reshape the influx of popular culture.

HOW CAN LOCAL AND POPULAR CULTURES BE SEEN IN THE LANDSCAPE?

29. The tension between globalized popular culture and local culture can be seen in _________ ______________, the visible imprint of human activity on the landscape.
30. As you drive down one of these roadways, one place looks like the _______. You drive past TGI Fridays, Applebee's, Walmart, Target, and ___________. Then, several miles down the road, you pass another _____________ (clustering) of the same stores. Geographer Edward Relph coined the word ___________ to describe the loss of __________ of place in the cultural landscape to the point that one place looks like the next.
31. Marked landscape similarities like these can be found everywhere from international airports to shopping centers. Global corporations that develop spaces of commerce have wide-reaching impacts on the cultural landscape.
32. In less obvious ways, cultural _________ and mixing are happening all around the world. This idea is behind the global _________ __________concept. This notion emphasizes that what happens at one scale is not independent of what happens at _______ scales.
33. People in a local place mediate and alter regional, national, and global processes, in a process called ______________.
34. Founders and early followers of the Church of Jesus Christ of Latter-day Saints created the Mormon landscape of the American ______ as they migrated westward under persecution and in search of a place where they could practice their religion _______.

Step 4: "Map It!" Quiz: Use the maps from the text to answer the questions.

1. According to Figure 4.5, which of the following states has a large concentration of Hutterites?
   A. Wisconsin
   B. Arkansas
   C. California
   D. South Dakota
   E. Utah

2. Which of the following is NOT a reason why there are so many Irish pubs in North America compared with South America (Figure 4.11)?
   A. North America has a more developed economy that is closely tied to commodification and globalization.
   B. South America's main religions forbid drinking alcohol in public places.
   C. The Irish migrated to North America in much larger numbers than to South America.
   D. Chain migration patterns help diffuse culture to North America more than to South America.
   E. General patterns of distance decay and the gravity model.

3. Which of the following regions has the largest number of buildings over 780 feet tall (Figure 4.23)?
   A. North America
   B. Russia
   C. Europe
   D. Southeast Asia
   E. East Asia

Step 5: AP-Style Practice Quiz

1. How do the Hutterites differ from the Amish?
   A. Hutterites wear clothing that is less traditional than the Amish.
   B. The Amish wear clothing that is less traditional than the Hutterites.
   C. Hutterite children will attend regular public schools.
   D. Hutterites readily accept technologies that help their agricultural work.
   E. The Amish readily accept technologies that help their agricultural work.

2. Little Sweden, the United States is an example of:
   A. globalization
   B. commodification
   C. neolocalism
   D. time–space compression
   E. placelessness

3. What are the two goals of local cultures?
   A. to commodify their material and nonmaterial culture
   B. to escape persecution and find a place to practice their religion
   C. to preserve tradition and assimilate with local residents
   D. to appropriate the customs of other cultures and make them authentically their own
   E. to keep other cultures out and keep their own culture in

4. What is the greatest challenge to urban local cultures?
   A. migration of "others" into their neighborhoods
   B. deterioration of housing stock
   C. discrimination by the mainstream culture
   D. dissemination of popular culture through media
   E. a younger generation not interested in the old ways

5. The rapid diffusion of innovations through modern technology that quickly links distant locations is known as:
   A. distance decay
   B. authenticity transmission
   C. reterritorialization
   D. time–space compression
   E. placelessness

6. The Mormon cultural region surrounds which of the following states?
   A. Pennsylvania
   B. Iowa
   C. Utah
   D. Oklahoma
   E. Kansas

7. What was the policy by which the U.S. government tried to make Native Americans more like Americans of European (white) descent?
   A. cultural appropriation
   B. ethnic reformation
   C. neolocalism
   D. assimilation
   E. commodification

8. Distance decay ensures that:
   A. the idea no longer spreads at a constant rate
   B. diseases and decay will spread faster
   C. better connected cities, regardless of distance, will receive innovations quicker than nearby but less connected locations
   D. the authenticity of a cultural trait decreases exponentially as it diffuses globally
   E. closer places are more likely to adopt innovations than places farther away

9. Which region of the world has the greatest number of skyscrapers?
   A. South America
   B. Europe
   C. North America
   D. South Asia
   E. East Asia

10. Which of the following is an example of cultural appropriation?
    A. extreme sports becoming mainstream sports
    B. Japan's adoption of Western technology in the late 1800s, but not the West's cultural values
    C. an American rural community descended from Germans deciding to have an annual German festival
    D. celebrities adopting some aspect of a local culture, resulting in that local culture becoming more accessible to popular culture trends
    E. the homogenization of the world's cultural landscape (McDonaldization)

CHAPTER 5:
IDENTITY: RACE, ETHNICITY, GENDER, AND SEXUALITY

Name: ______________________________**Period** __________**Date**____________

Chapter Title: ____

Chapter # ____________________________**Pgs.** ___________**to** ___________

The Five Steps to Chapter Success

Step 1: Read the Chapter Summary below and preview the Key Questions.
Step 2: Complete the Pre-Reading Activity (PRA) for this chapter.
Step 3: Read the chapter and complete the guided worksheet.
Step 4: Read the maps and take the "Map It!"quiz
Step 5: Take an AP-style Practice Quiz

STEP 1: Chapter Summary and Key Questions

Chapter Summary

Identity is a powerful concept. The way we make sense of ourselves is a personal journey that is mediated and influenced by the political, social, and cultural contexts in which we live and work. Group identities such as gender, ethnicity, race, and sexuality are constructed, both by self-realization and by identifying against and across scales. When learning about new places and different people, humans are often tempted to put places and people into boxes, into myths or stereotypes that make them easily digestible.

The geographer, especially one who spends time in the field, recognizes that how people shape and create places varies across time and space and that time, space, and place shape people, both individually and in groups. James Curtis ably described the work of a geographer who studies places: "But like the popular images and stereotypical portrayals of all places—whether positive or negative, historical or contemporary—these mask a reality on the ground that is decidedly more complex and dynamic, from both the economic and social perspectives." What Curtis says about places is true about people as well. What we may think to be positive identities, such as the myths of "Orientalism" or of the "model minority," and what we know are negative social ills, such as racism and dowry deaths, are all decidedly more complex and dynamic than they first seem.

Key Questions

Field Note: Building Walls	p. 117–118
1. What is identity, and how are identities constructed?	p. 119–126
2. How do places affect identity, and how do we see identities?	p. 127–130
3. How does geography reflect and shape power relationships among groups of people?	p. 130–141

Step 2: Pre-Reading Activity (PRA)

1. Write down each of the Key Questions with the fewest pages and the most pages.

Key Question	# of Pages

2. After looking over the Key Questions and the Chapter Summary, write a few sentences about what you expect to learn in general in this chapter.

3. How many world maps are there in this chapter? _____ (Go to Student Companion Website and print out organizers for help.)

4. Read the Field Note introduction of the chapter and list three specific facts you learned.

____

____

____

____

____

____

____

5. Go to Step 1 and look at the Geographic Concepts. Create a list of terms you think you know and terms you need to know.

I THINK I KNOW	I NEED TO LEARN

Step 3: Chapter 5 Guided Worksheet

Directions: As you read the chapter, fill in the blanks on the guided worksheet.

FIELDWORK—BUILDING WALLS

1. The woman in Figure 5.1 worked ____ hours a day, six days a week, turning, stacking, and restacking bricks to prevent them from ___________.
2. More than a century ago, bricks were made this way in the ________ ___________. Today, the brick-making industry in the United States makes use of a great deal of ___________ and robotics to manufacture bricks.
3. Geographers Mona Domosh and Joni Seager define _________ as "a culture's assumptions about the ___________ between men and women: their 'characters,' the roles they play in society, what they represent." Divisions of _______ are one of the clearest ways in which societies are gendered.
4. In Bali, brick-making is still done by hand by boys and ________.

WHAT IS IDENTITY, AND HOW ARE IDENTITIES CONSTRUCTED?

5. Geographer Gillian Rose defines identity as "how we make ________ of ourselves." How do we each _________ ourselves? We construct our own identities through experiences, emotions, connections, and ___________. An identity is a ___________, an image of who we are at that moment. Identities are _______, constantly changing, shifting, and becoming.
6. One of the most powerful ways to construct an identity is by identifying ___________ other people. To identify against, we first define the "Other," and then we define ourselves in ___________ terms.
7. The various "races" people identify are tied to __________ attributes of humans that have developed over time as modern humans spread around the world. Closer to the poles, humans developed __________ skin pigment so that skin could absorb sunlight that bodies could convert into vitamin ____ during the half of the year when the region received sunlight.

8. Unlike a local culture or ethnicity to which we may choose to belong, _______ is an identity that is more often _____________.
9. Because of the redesignation of _________ as an ethnicty, in the boxes provided by the United States Census Bureau a person can now be “White, non-Hispanic,” “White, Hispanic,” “Black, non-Hispanic,” “Black, Hispanic,” and so forth.
10. Geographers Douglas Massey and Nancy Denton defined __________ ____________ as the “degree to which two or more groups live separately from one another, in different parts of the _________ environment.”
11. In 2010, the most residentially segregated large metropolitan area for African Americans was ____________, Wisconsin
12. We have different identities at different ________: individual, local, regional, national, and global.
13. New immigrants to a city often move to __________ areas that are being gradually abandoned by older immigrant groups. This process is called __________. In New York, ________ ________ moved into the immigrant Jewish neighborhood of East Harlem in the early twentieth century, successively assuming a dominant presence in the neighborhood.

HOW DO PLACES AFFECT IDENTITY, AND HOW CAN WE SEE IDENTITIES IN PLACES?

14. Like identity, our sense of place is _______; it changes as the place changes and as we change.
15. ___________ offers a good example of how identities affect places and how places affect identities. The idea of ethnicity as an identity stems from the notion that people are closely bounded, even _________, in a certain place over time. The word “ethnic” comes from the ancient Greek word ________, meaning “people” or “nation.”
16. The town of _________ is the capital of the State of Baja California. Not far from the central business district of Mexicali lies one of the largest ______________ in Mexico.
17. ___________ Chinatown is experiencing a transformation, as Chinese residents have dispersed to the ______ of the city and beyond (many because they can afford to move out of town now). Relatively _____ Chinese continue to live in the city’s Chinatown; some have even moved across the border to Calexico (a city of 27,000 on the California side of the border), while retaining ________ interests in Mexicali.
18. Doreen Massey and Pat Jess define space as “________ _________ stretched out” and place as “particular articulations of those social relations as they have come together, over time, in that particular location.”
19. We can, for example, create places that are __________—places seen as being appropriate for women or for men.

HOW DOES GEOGRAPHY REFLECT AND SHAPE POWER RELATIONSHIPS AMONG GROUPS?

20. __________ relationships are assumptions and structures about who is in ________ and who has power over others. Power relationships affect __________ directly, and the nature of those effects depends on the geographical context in which they are situated.

21. The _____________ governments collect and report reflect the power relationships involved in defining what is valued and what is not. Think back to the Constitution of the United States prior to the Fourteenth Amendment, when the government enumerated a black person as ___________ of a white person.

22. Throughout the world, the work of __________ is often undervalued and uncounted. Scholars estimate that if women's productivity in the household alone were given a dollar value by calculating what it would cost to hire people to perform these tasks, the gross national income (GNI) for all countries of the world combined would ________ by about _____________.

23. Statistics showing how much women produce and how _______ their work is valued are undoubtedly interesting.

24. Migration flows, birth rates, and child mortality rates affect the _________ ___________ of cities, states, and regions.

25. In the large region of _____________ Africa, women outnumber men in many rural areas. Women in Subsaharan Africa have heavy responsibilities, coupled in many places with few rights and ________ ______. Women produce an estimated _____ percent of the region's food, almost all of it _____________ the aid of modern technology.

26. Rather, another African country, _____________, is the first country in the world where women hold more than _____ percent of the legislative seats. Rwanda suffered a bloody ________ _______ in the 1990s in which over 800,000 people died (one-tenth of the population at the time), a majority of whom were ______. Immediately after the war, _________ accounted for more than 70 percent of the population of the country.

27. On a 2004 *Oprah!* show, the talk show hostess interviewed journalist Lisa Ling about her travels through _________ and her reports on _________ _______ in India. The Chicago audience looked stunned to discover that thousands of girls in India are still betrothed through arranged marriages and that in some extreme cases, disputes over the dowry, which is the price to be paid by the bride's family to the groom's father, have led to the _______ of the bride.

28. In California and in much of the rest of the United States, the "Asian" box is drawn around a stereotype of what some call the "_________ _________." Frazier and his colleagues explain the myth of the model minority: The myth "paints Asians as good, hardworking people who, despite their suffering through ___________, harassment, and exclusion, have found ways to __________ through peaceful means."

29. Over the last four decades, the greatest migration flow into California and the southwestern United States has come from __________ ______________ and the Caribbean, especially __________.

30. In his study of the region, Curtis records the changes to the __________ ___________ in the process. He uses the term ________________ (derived from the Spanish word for

neighborhood, barrio) to describe a change that saw the Hispanic population of a neighborhood jump from 4 percent in 1960 to over _____ percent in 2000.

31. On April 29–30, 1992, _____ ____________ became engulfed in one of the worst incidents of civil unrest in United States history. During two days of ___________ 43 people died, 2383 were injured, and 16,291 arrested.

32. They found that the population of the area was over 90 percent _________ __________ in 1970, but by 1990, the population was evenly split between African Americans and ___________. This change in population composition was accompanied by a steady influx of _________ residents and small _________ owners seeking a niche in the rapidly changing urban area

33. Johnson and his colleagues argued that the Los Angeles riots were more than a spontaneous _________ to a verdict. They were rooted in the growing despair and frustration of different ethnic groups competing for a _______ number of ______ in an environment of declining housing conditions and scarce public resources.

Step 4: "Map It" Quiz: Use the maps from the text to answer the questions.

1. Which of these regions has the lowest gender inequality (Figure 5.15)?
   A. North America
   B. Europe
   C. East Asia
   D. Austral region
   E. Russia

2. Which of these regions has the highest gender inequality (Figure 5.15)?
   A. South America
   B. East Asia
   C. South Asia
   D. Southeast Asia
   E. North Africa and Southwest Asia

3. Which of the following countries had less than 40 percent of women in national legislatures (Figure 5.17)?
   A. Ecuador
   B. Finland
   C. Sweden
   D. Nicaragua
   E. the United States

4. Which of the following countries had less than 10 percent of women in national legislatures (Figure 5.17)?
   A. Russia
   B. Iran
   C. Cuba
   D. China
   E. South Africa

Step 5: AP-Style Practice Quiz

1. How does "ethnicity" differ from "race?"
   A. There is no difference in common usage.
   B. Ethnicity implies a religious affiliation; race does not.
   C. Ideas of ethnicity and race have not changed over time.
   D. Race is something to which we choose to belong; ethnicity is assigned.
   E. Ethnicity is something to which we choose to belong; race is assigned.

2. Which of the following is NOT a reason why factory managers employ young women in large numbers in poor countries?
   A. Women are less likely to form unions and strike.
   B. Women are more adept at doing repetitive tasks.
   C. Women are more easily exploited.
   D. Women are comparatively free from family responsibilities.
   E. Women are paid higher wages for their work.

3. State of mind derived through the infusion of a place with meaning and emotion is called
   A. sense of place
   B. ethnicity
   C. ethnic space
   D. queer theory
   E. immigrants

4. Who produces about 70 percent of the food in rural Subsaharan Africa?
   A. men
   B. women
   C. children
   D. agribusiness companies
   E. immigrants

5. Barrioization refers to:
   A. the increasing political clout of Mexican immigrants in big-city politics
   B. the replacement of Anglo-American street names with Spanish street names
   C. neighborhoods, especially in Los Angeles, where the Hispanic population rapidly displaces the original residents
   D. the gerrymandering of voting districts in predominantly Hispanic regions
   E. states where Hispanics will represent a majority population in the next 20 years

6. The most residentially segregated large metropolitan area for African Americans is:
   A. Detroit, Michigan
   B. Orange County, California
   C. San Francisco, California
   D. Milwaukee, Wisconsin
   E. New York, New York

7. In New York, Puerto Ricans took over Jewish neighborhoods in a process geographers call:
   A. residential segregation
   B. ethnic succession
   C. residential invasion
   D. cultural transition
   E. invasion and succession

8. What would happen to the world's gross national income if the work women do at home was calculated at market value?
   A. There is no way to accurately estimate the value of such work.
   B. Global GNI would remain the same.
   C. Global GNI would actually decline.
   D. Global GNI would grow by 10 percent.
   E. Global GNI would grow by about one-third.

9. How has the town of Mexicali changed over time?
   A. More Chinese have immigrated to Mexicali.
   B. Mexicans have moved out of the city of Mexicali.
   C. Mexicali no longer has Chinese businesses.
   D. The Chinese have moved to the edges of the city and neighboring towns.
   E. The town hasn't change in nearly 20 years.

10. What is a term used in the discussion of sexual behavior, gender, and society, primarily within the fields of queer theory and gender theory? It is used to describe (and frequently to criticize) the manner in which many social institutions and social policies are seen to reinforce certain beliefs.
    A. transgender
    B. sexual identity
    C. gendered roles
    D. identity
    E. heteronormative

CHAPTER 6:
LANGUAGE

Name: Sanya **Period** 7 **Date** ____________
Chapter Title: ____
Chapter # ____________________ **Pgs.** ____________ **to** ____________

The Five Steps to Chapter Success

Step 1: Read the Chapter Summary below and preview the Key Questions.
Step 2: Complete the Pre-Reading Activity (PRA) for this chapter.
Step 3: Read the chapter and complete the guided worksheet.
Step 4: Read the maps and take the "Map It!"quiz
Step 5: Take an AP-style Practice Quiz

STEP 1: Chapter Summary and Key Questions

Chapter Summary

The global mosaic of languages reflects centuries of divergence, convergence, extinction, and diffusion. Linguists and linguistic geographers have the interesting work of uncovering, through deep reconstruction, the hearths of the world's language families. Some languages, such as Basque, defy explanation. Other languages are the foci of countless studies, many of which come to differing conclusions about their ancient origins.

As certain languages, such as English and Chinese, gain speakers and become global languages, other languages become extinct. Some languages come to serve as the lingua franca of a region or place. Governments choose official languages, and through public schools, educators entrench an official language in a place. Some countries, faced with the global diffusion of the English language, defend and promote their national language. Whether requiring signs to be written a certain way or requiring a television station to broadcast some proportion of programming in the national language, governments can preserve language, choose a certain dialect as the standard, or repel the diffusion of other languages.

Regardless of the place, the people, or the language used, language continues to define, shape, and maintain culture. How a person thinks about the world is reflected in the words used to describe and define it.

Key Questions

Field Note: What Should I Say?	p.144–147
1. What are languages, and what role do languages play in cultures?)	p.147–153 6
2. Why are languages distributed the way they are?	p.153–161 8
3. How did certain languages become dominant?	p.162–165 3
4. What role does language play in making places?	p.165–170 5

Step 2: Pre-Reading Activity (PRA)

1. Write down each of the Key Questions with the fewest pages and the most pages.

Key Question	# of Pages
Why are languages distributed the way they are?	8
HOw did artain languaged become dominant?	3

2. After looking over the Key Questions and the Chapter Summary, write a few sentences about what you expect to learn in general in this chapter.

I expect to learn about the diffusion of language. Furthermore, I will learn about the dominant languages of different regions.

3. How many world maps are there in this chapter? 1 (Go to Student Companion Website and print out organizers for help.)

4. Read the Field Note introduction of the chapter and list three specific facts you learned.

1. Belgium speaks 3 dominant languages: French, Flemish and German.

2. Language conflict are often political.

3. No national political parties in Belgium.

5 Go to Step 1 and look at the Geographic Concepts. Create a list of terms you think you know and terms you need to know.

I THINK I KNOW	I NEED TO LEARN
Language	isogloss
official language	conquest theory
place	Proto-Eurasiatic
extinct language	Creole language

Step 3: Chapter 6 Guided Worksheet

Directions: As you read the chapter, fill in the blanks on the guided worksheet.

FIELD NOTE—WHAT SHOULD I SAY?

1. In stores throughout Brussels, Belgium, you can see the capital city's bilingualism all around you—literally. From McDonald's to health insurance offices to the metro, signs in Brussels are posted in duplicate, with one in Flemish (a variant of Dutch) and one in French.
2. Look at the European map of languages, and zero in on Belgium. The map shows a neat line dividing Flemish speakers (a Germanic language) in the northern region of Flanders from French speakers (a Romance language) in the southern region of Wallonia.
3. Behind this neat line on the language map is a complicated, at times contentious, linguistic transition zone. Although the bilingual capital of Brussels is located in the Flemish-speaking north (Flanders), for upwards of 80 percent of the locals, French is the mother tongue.
4. The example of Belgium gives us a multitude of insights into language. Language questions are often politicized. Language frequently is tied to other identity issues, and socioeconomic divisions can exacerbate tensions between language groups. At the same time, the role of English continues to expand as the dominant language of global commerce, electronic communication, and popular culture.

WHAT ARE LANGUAGES, AND WHAT ROLE DO LANGUAGES PLAY IN CULTURES?

5. Language is a fundamental element of local and national culture. The French government has worked diligently, even aggressively, to protect the French language, dating back to 1635 and the creation of the Académie Française, an institution charged with standardizing and protecting the French language.

6. With the support of many French people, the French government passed a law in 1975 banning the use of foreign words in advertisements, television, and radio broadcasts, as well as official documents, unless no French equivalent could be found.
7. A language is a set of sounds and symbols that is used for communication.
8. Language can reveal much about the way people and cultures view reality. For example, some African languages have no word or term for the concept of a god.
9. In Quebec, Canada, the focus is on passing laws that promote the use of the province's distinct version of the French language. Canada is officially bilingual, a reflection of the colonial division of the country between France and Great Britain.
10. Many geography textbooks differentiate languages based on a criterion of mutual intelligibility. Mutual intelligibility means that two people can understand each other when speaking. The argument goes that if two of us are speaking two different languages, say Spanish and Portuguese, we will not be able to understand each other, but if we are speaking two dialects of one language, we will achieve mutual understanding.
11. Language is dynamic: New discoveries, technologies, and ideas require new words. Technologically advanced societies are likely to have a standard language, one that is published, widely distributed, and purposely taught.
12. Variants of a standard language along regional or ethnic lines are called dialects. Differences in vocabulary, syntax (the way words are put together to form phrases), pronunciation, cadence (the rhythm of speech), and even the pace of speech all mark a speaker's dialect.
13. Frequently, dialects are marked by actual differences in vocabulary. A single word or group of words can reveal the source area of the dialect. Linguistic geographers map the extent of particular words, marking their limits as isoglosses. An isogloss is a geographic boundary within which a particular linguistic feature occurs, but such a boundary is rarely a simple line.

WHY ARE LANGUAGES DISTRIBUTED THE WAY THEY ARE?

14. At the global scale, we classify languages into language families. Each family encompasses multiple languages that have a shared but fairly distant origin. We break language families into subfamilies (divisions within a language family), where the commonalities are more definite and their origin is more recent.
15. Even when it comes to individual languages, complicated issues arise. English is the most widely spoken Indo-European language; its speakers encircle the world with more than 350 million in North America, 60 million in Britain and Ireland, 205 million in Australia and New Zealand, and tens of millions more in South Africa, India, and elsewhere in the postcolonial world. Hundreds of millions of people speak versions of English as a second or third language.
16. If we look carefully at the map of world language families, some interesting questions arise. Consider, for example, the island of Madagascar off the East African coast. The primary languages people in Madagascar speak belong not to an African language family but to the Austronesian family, the languages of Southeast Asia and the Pacific Islands.

17. From Jones's notions and Grimm's ideas came the first major linguistic hypothesis, proposing the existence of an ancestral Indo-European language called Proto-Indo-European, which in turn gave rise to modern languages from Scandinavia to North Africa and from North America through parts of Asia to Australia.
18. Languages do not change solely through divergence (the splitting of branches); they also change through convergence and extinction. If peoples with different languages have consistent spatial interaction, language convergence can take place, collapsing two languages into one.
19. Language extinction creates branches on the tree with dead ends, representing a halt in interaction between the extinct language and languages that continued.
20. Indo-European spread from its hearth westward into Europe and eastward into what is now Iran, Pakistan, and India.
21. The conquest theory provides one explanation for the dominance of Indo-European tongues in the wake of these migrations. This theory holds that early speakers of Proto-Indo-European spread from east to west on horseback, overpowering earlier inhabitants and beginning the diffusion and differentiation of Indo-European tongues.
22. An alternative agricultural theory proposes that Proto-Indo-European spread with the diffusion of agriculture.
23. The Romance languages (French, Spanish, Italian, Romanian, and Portuguese) lie in the areas of Europe that were once controlled by the Roman Empire.
24. The Germanic languages (English, German, Danish, Norwegian, and Swedish) reflect the expansion of peoples out of Northern Europe to the west and south. The Germanic character of English bears the imprint of a further migration—that of the Normans into England in 1066, bringing a Romance tongue to the British Isles.
25. The Slavic languages (Russian, Polish, Czech, Slovak, Ukrainian, Slovenian, Serbo-Croatian, and Bulgarian) developed as Slavic people migrated from a base in present-day Ukraine close to 2000 years ago.
26. In some places, however, linguistic and political borders are far from coincident. The French linguistic region extends into Belgium, Switzerland, and Italy, but in France, French coexists with Basque in the southwest, a variant of Dutch in the north, and a Celtic tongue in the northwest.
27. One language on the map of Europe stands out for two reasons: First, it covers a very small land area, and second, it is in no way related to any other language family in Europe. This tantalizing enigma is the Basque language, Euskera. Isolated in the Andorra Mountain region between Spain and France, the Basque people and their Euskera language survived the tumultuous history of Europe for thousands of years—never blending with another language or diffusing from the Andorra region.
28. Were it not for British colonialism, the country of Nigeria would never have existed. When Nigeria gained its independence in 1962, the government decided to adopt English as the "official" language, as the three major regional languages are too politically charged and thus unsuitable as national languages.

HOW DO CERTAIN LANGUAGES BECOME DOMINANT?

29. Just a few thousand years ago, most habitable parts of Earth were characterized by a tremendous diversity of languages. In the late Middle Ages, the invention of the Gutenberg printing press and the rise of nation-states worked to spread literacy and stabilize certain languages through widely distributed written forms.
30. A lingua franca is a language used among speakers of different languages for the purposes of trade and commerce. A lingua franca can be a single language, or it can be a mixture of two or more languages. When people speaking two or more languages are in contact and they combine parts of their languages in a simplified structure and vocabulary, we call it a pidgin language.
31. A different sort of a lingua franca in wide use today is Swahili, the lingua franca of East Africa.
32. Over time a pidgin language may gain native speakers, becoming the first language children learn in the home. When this happens, we call it a creolized or Creole language. A Creole language is a pidgin language that has developed a more complex structure and vocabulary and has become the native language of a group of people.

WHAT ROLE DOES LANGUAGE PLAY IN MAKING PLACES?

33. To be sure, a few virtually monolingual states—countries where almost everyone speaks the same language—do exist. These include Japan in Asia; Uruguay in South America; Iceland, Denmark, Portugal, and Poland in Europe; and Lesotho in Africa.
34. Countries in which more than one language is in use are called multilingual states.
35. Countries with linguistic fragmentation often adopt an official language (or languages) to tie the people together.
36. More and more people are using English in a variety of contexts. English is now the standard language of international business and travel (the lingua franca), much of contemporary popular culture bears the imprint of English, and the computer and telecommunications revolution relies heavily on the use of English terminology.
37. Yet if global language means a common language of trade and commerce used around the world, the picture looks rather different.
38. Each place has a unique location and constitutes a reflection of human activities, ideas, and tangible, durable creations.
39. Geographers call place-names toponyms. Such names often refer to the social processes going on in a particular area, and these may determine whether a toponym is passed down or changed, how the people will interpret the history of a place, and how the people will see a place.
40. In his book, *Names on the Land: A Historical Account of Place-Naming in the United States* (1982), English professor George Stewart recognized that certain themes dominate American toponyms. Stewart developed a classification scheme focused on _____ basic types of place-names, including: descriptive (Rocky Mountains), commendatory (Paradise Valley, Arizona), and possession (Johnson City, Texas).

41. Most Brazilian toponyms are Portuguese, reflecting the Portuguese colonization of the land.
42. The toponyms we see on a map depend in large part on who produced the map.
43. The question of changing toponyms often arises when power changes hands in a place. When African colonies became independent countries, many of the new governments immediately changed the toponyms of places named after colonial figures.
44. Newly independent countries also changed the names of cities, towns, and geographic features to reflect their independence. Thus, Leopoldville (named after a Belgian king) became kinshasa, capital of the Congo; Salisbury, Zimbabwe, named after a British leader, became Harare; and Lourenço Marques, Mozambique, commemorating a Portuguese naval hero, became Maputo.
45. Independence prompts name changes, and so too do changes in power through coups and revolutions. During his reign, authoritarian dictator General Mobuto Sese Seko changed the name of the Belgian Congo in Subsaharan Africa to Zaire.
46. People can choose to change a toponym to memorialize an important person or event. Hundreds of parks in the United States are named Memorial Park to commemorate a person or event.
47. Alderman studied the practice of changing street names to memorialize Martin Luther King Jr. (MLK), the major African American leader of the civil rights movement.
48. Although streets named after MLK are found throughout the United States, the greatest concentration of memorial streets are in the South, especially in Georgia (King's home state) and Mississippi.
49. In recent years, the activities of corporations with a global reach have been stamped on the landscape. Stadiums are especially susceptible to this form of commodification: FedEx Field, Verizon Center, TD Bank Garden, CenturyLink Field, and Coors Field are perfect examples.

Step 4: "Map It" Quiz: Use the maps from the text to answer the questions.

1. Which Indo-European language branch dominates eastern Europe (Figure 6.2)?
   A. Romance
   B. Germanic
   C. Celtic
   D. Uralic
   (E.) Slavic

2. Which of the following states uses "pop" as a common name for a soft drink (Figure 6.7)?
   A. Texas
   (B.) Illinois
   C. New York
   D. California
   E. Florida

3. What language family dominates North, Middle and South America (Figure 6.8)?
   A. Afro-Asiatic
   B. Amerindian
   C. Indo-European
   D. Sino-Tibetan
   E. Uralic

4. What language family dominates Southern India (Figure 6.8)?
   A. Dravidian
   B. Indo-European
   C. Sino-Tibetan
   D. Uralic
   E. Austronesian

5. What language family dominates North Africa and Southwest Asia (Figure 6.8)?
   A. Dravidian
   B. Afro-Asiatic
   C. Indo-European
   D. Sino-Tibetan
   E. Urali

6. If you understand the population of Australia correctly, it is obvious that the ____________ family dominates the cultural landscape (Figure 6.8).
   A. Dravidian
   B. Austronesian
   C. Indo-European
   D. Sino-Tibetan
   E. Dravidian

Step 5: AP-Style Practice Quiz

1. The predominant languages spoken on Madagascar are not of an African language family but belong to a(n):
   A. Indo-European family
   B. Sino-Tibetan family
   C. Dravidian family
   D. Austronesian family
   E. Altaic family

2. A geographic boundary within which a particular linguistic feature occurs is called a(n):
   A. isotherm
   B. sound shift
   C. international border
   D. cultural boundary
   E. isogloss

3. Which of the following European countries has a rather sharp division between Flemish speakers in the north and Walloon speakers in the south?
   A. The Netherlands
   B. Belgium
   C. Denmark
   D. Andorra
   E. Switzerland

4. The Indo-European language family prevails on the map of Europe. Which country listed below has a language that is not in the Indo-European family?
   A. France
   B. Italy
   C. Iceland
   D. Luxembourg
   E. Hungary

5. Bantu migrations marginalized this once widespread African language family that now is found only in dry regions of southwestern Africa.
   A. Niger-Congo family
   B. Khoisan family
   C. Afro-Asiatic family
   D. Sudanic subfamily
   E. Gaelic subfamily

6. In an attempt to deal with linguistic as well as cultural diversity, many former African colonies have taken as their official language:
   A. the most widely spoken indigenous language
   B. an Austronesian and therefore neutral language
   C. the language of the former colonial power
   D. an invented language with no historical connections
   E. Swahili, the lingua franca of all of Africa

7. When African colonies became independent countries, one of the first acts of many of the new governments was to:
   A. conduct a census
   B. build a new capital city
   C. change the names of places that had been named after colonial figures
   D. build new road systems
   E. seek international aid

8. In technically advanced societies, there is likely to be:
   A. a standard language
   B. many basic languages
   C. limited expansion of language
   D. standard pronunciation
   E. a lot of technical terms

9. According to the text, dialects are usually marked by differences in all of the following EXCEPT:
   A. accents
   B. pronunciation
   C. vocabulary
   D. syntax
   E. diction

10. Convergence processes yielding a synthesis of several languages produce a pidgin language. When this language becomes the first language of a population, it is referred to as a:
    A. dialect
    B. Creole language
    C. language subfamily
    D. lingua franca
    E. corrupted language

CHAPTER 7:
RELIGION

Name: ______________________________ **Period** __________ **Date** __________

Chapter Title: ____

Chapter # ______________________________ **Pgs.** __________ **to** __________

The Five Steps to Chapter Success

Step 1: Read the Chapter Summary below and preview the Key Questions.
Step 2: Complete the Pre-Reading Activity (PRA) for this chapter.
Step 3: Read the chapter and complete the guided worksheet.
Step 4: Read the maps and take the "Map It!"quiz
Step 5: Take an AP-style Practice Quiz

STEP 1: Chapter Summary and Key Questions

Chapter Summary

Religion is a major force in shaping and changing culture. The major world religions today all stem from an area of Eurasia stretching from the eastern Mediterranean to China. Major world religions are distributed regionally, with Hinduism in India; Buddhism, Taoism, Shintoism, and Chinese philosophies in East and Southeast Asia; Islam reaching across North Africa, through the Middle East and into Southeast Asia; Shamanist religions mainly in Subsaharan Africa; and Christianity in Europe, Western Asia, the Americas, Australia, and New Zealand. Judaism, another major world religion, is not as concentrated. Today, Judaism has a base in Israel and has adherents scattered throughout Europe and the Americas.

As the 2014 Boko haram kidnapping of 250 teenage girls in Nigeria made clear, religious beliefs can drive people to extremist behaviors. On a day-to-day basis, however, religion more typically drives cultures—shaping how people behave, how people perceive the behaviors of others, and how people across place, scale, and time interact with each other.

Key Questions

Field Note: Peace Walls	p. 171–172
1. What is religion, and what role does it play in culture?	p. 172–175
2. Where did the major religions of the world originate, and how do religions diffuse?	p. 175–190
3. How is religion seen in the cultural landscape?	p.190–199
4. What role does religion play in political conflicts?	p. 200–210

Step 2: Pre-Reading Activity (PRA)

1. Write down each of the Key Questions with the fewest pages and the most pages.

Key Question	# of Pages

2. After looking over the Key Questions and the Chapter Summary, write a few sentences about what you expect to learn in general in this chapter.

3. How many world maps are there in this chapter? _____ (Go to Student Companion Website and print out organizers for help.)

4. Read the Field Note introduction of the chapter and list three specific facts you learned.

6 Go to Step 1 and look at the Geographic Concepts. Create a list of terms you think you know and terms you need to know.

I THINK I KNOW	I NEED TO LEARN

Step 3: Chapter 7 Guided Worksheet

Directions: As you read the chapter, fill in the blanks on the guided worksheet.

FIELD NOTE—PEACE WALLS

1. A 40-foot-tall ________ ______ towered behind the gardens, and next to the garden stretching along the wall was a row of houses settled by ___________. On the other side of the peace wall was the ____________ Shankhill neighborhood, where I had been 10 minutes earlier.
2. The peace walls are quite visible, but the residents of this area of Belfast also carry invisible lines in their minds of routes that are _____ and paths that are ____.
3. Boal found that members of each group traveled _________ distances to shop in grocery stores tagged as their respective religion, walked further to catch a bus in a neighborhood belonging to their own religion, gave their neighborhood different toponyms, read different newspapers, and cheered for different ___________ (soccer) teams.
4. In the journal *Children's Geographies*, Madeleine Leonard (2006) studied how teens in ________ negotiate living in interfaith areas where Catholic and Protestant neighborhoods meet and where violence and trauma occurred.

WHAT IS RELIGION, AND WHAT ROLE DOES IT PLAY IN CULTURE?

5. __________ and language lie at the foundation of culture: Both confer and reflect identity. Like languages, religions are constantly ___________.
6. The ___________ ____________ is marked by religion—most obviously by churches, synagogues, temples, and __________, cemeteries and shrines, statues and symbols.
7. Geographers Robert Stoddard and Carolyn Prorak define religion as "a system of _________ and practices that attempts to order life in terms of culturally perceived ultimate _____________".

8. Although religious beliefs and prescriptions influence many societies, in other places, religion, at least in its organized form, has become ________ ____________ in the lives of people. Secularism is the indifference to or rejection of formal religion. The most secular countries in the world today are in _________.

WHERE DID THE MAJOR RELIGIONS OF THE WORLD ORIGINATE, AND HOW DO RELIGIONS DIFFUSE?

9. Adherents of monotheistic religions worship a ________ deity, a God ("Allah" in Arabic). Believers in ___________ religions worship more than one deity, even thousands. ___________ religions are centered on the belief that inanimate objects, such as mountains, boulders, rivers, and trees, possess spirits and should therefore be revered.
10. Somewhere around 3500 years ago, however, a monotheistic religion developed in Southwest Asia called ______________.
11. By 500 BCE, four major _________ of religion and philosophy had developed in the world. From a hearth in South Asia, along the _______ River Valley, came Hinduism; from a hearth on the eastern Mediterranean came __________; from a hearth on the _________ ___ (Yellow River) Valley in China came Chinese philosophies; and from the northern shores of the Mediterranean Sea came Greek philosophy.
12. Despite the limitations of the map of world religions, it illustrates how ____ Christian religions have diffused (2.2 billion adherents worldwide), the extent of the _________ of Islam (1.6 billion), the connection between Hinduism (950 million adherents) and one of the world's major population concentrations, and the continued importance of Buddhism (347 million followers) in parts of Asia.
13. _____________ religions actively seek converts because they view themselves as offering belief systems of universal appropriateness and appeal. ________________, Islam, and Buddhism all fall within this category, and their universalizing character helps explain their widespread distribution.
14. In an ________ religion, adherents are born into the faith and converts are not actively sought. Ethnic religions (405 million followers) tend to be spatially ____________—as is the case with traditional religions, which are found primarily in small areas of Asia, the Pacific, Africa, and ________ ____________.
15. In terms of number of adherents, Hinduism ranks ________ after Christianity and Islam as a world religion. Hinduism has over 1 billion adherents and is one of the oldest religions in the modern world, dating back over 4000 years, originating in the ______ River Valley of what is today part of Pakistan.
16. The fundamental doctrine is ______, which has to do with the transferability of the soul. According to Hindu doctrine, all beings have ______ and are arranged in a hierarchy. The ideal is to move upward in the hierarchy and then escape from the eternal cycle of _____________ through union with Brahman (the universal soul).
17. The _________ ___________locks people into particular social classes and imposes many restrictions, especially in the lowest of the castes and in those considered beneath the caste system, Dalits.
18. ________________ splintered from Hinduism over 2500 years ago.

19. Today Buddhism is practiced by relatively _____ in India, but it thrives in Sri Lanka, _____________ _____, Nepal, Tibet, and Korea.
20. Buddhism's various branches have an estimated 488 million adherents, with ___________, Theravada, and Vajrayana (Tibetan) Buddhism claiming the most adherents.
21. Buddhism is mixed with a local religion in Japan, where __________ is found.
22. The beginnings of _________ are unclear, but scholars trace the religion to an older contemporary of Confucius, _________, who published a volume titled Tao-te-ching, or "Book of the Way." In his teachings, Lao-Tsu focused on the proper form of political rule and on the oneness of humanity and ________: People, he said, should learn to live in harmony with nature. This idea gave rise to the concept of ________ _____—the art and science of organizing living spaces in order to channel the life forces that exist in nature in favorable ways.
23. Confucianism is mainly a ____________ of life, and like Taoism, it had great and lasting impacts on Chinese life.
24. ________ grew out of the belief system of the Jews, one of several nomadic Semitic tribes living in Southwest Asia about 4000 years ago. The roots of Jewish religious tradition lie in the teachings of ____________ (from Ur), who is credited with uniting his people to worship only one God.
25. The scattering of Jews after the Roman destruction of Jerusalem is known as the _________—a term that now signifies the spatial dispersion of members of any ethnic group. The Jews who went north into ________ __________ came to be known as Ashkenazim, and the Jews who scattered across North Africa and into the Iberian Peninsula (Spain and Portugal) are called Sephardim.
26. The idea of a homeland for the Jewish people, which became popular during the nineteenth century, developed into the ideology of _________. Zionist ideals are rooted in the belief that Jews should not be _________ into other societies.
27. _____________ can be traced back to the same hearth in the Mediterranean as Judaism, and like Judaism, Christianity stems from a single founder—in this case Jesus.
28. The first split in Christianity, between Roman Catholicism and the ________ _________ Church, developed over a number of centuries.
29. The Roman Catholic Church claims the _______ adherents of all Christian denominations (more than 1 billion).
30. Christianity is the largest and globally the most ________ dispersed religion.
31. __________ began in several parts of western Europe and expanded to some degree through contagious diffusion.
32. Like Christianity, Islam, the ___________ of the major religions, can be traced back to a single founder, in this case, Muhammad, who was born in Mecca in 570 CE.
33. Adherents to Islam are required to observe the __________ of Islam (repeated expressions of the basic creed, frequent prayer, a month of daytime fasting, almsgiving, and, if possible, at least one pilgrimage to Mecca in one's lifetime). The faith dictates behavior in other spheres of life as well. Islam forbids _________, smoking, and gambling.
34. Islam, like all other major religions, is ___________— principally between Sunni Muslims (the great majority) and the Shi'ite or Shiah Muslims (concentrated in Iran).

35. The religion's main division between _______ and _______ occurred almost immediately after Muhammad's death and was caused by a conflict over his succession.
36. Through _________, Muslims later spread their faith across the Indian Ocean into Southeast Asia.
37. Today, Islam, with more than 1.6 billion followers, ranks ________ to Christianity in global number of adherents. Islam is the ___________ growing of the world's major religions, dominating in Northern Africa and Southwest Asia, extending into Central Asia, the former Soviet Union and China, and including clusters in _____________, Bangladesh, and southern Mindanao in the Philippines.
38. ____________ religions are local in scope, usually have a reverence for nature, and are passed down through family units and groups (tribes) of indigenous peoples.
39. Shamanism is a community faith in which people follow their _________—a religious leader, teacher, healer, and visionary.
40. In many areas labeled Christian on the world map of religions, from Canada to Australia and from the United States to western Europe, the ________ of organized religion as a cultural force is evident.

HOW IS RELIGION SEEN IN THE CULTURAL LANDSCAPE?

41. When adherents voluntarily travel to a religious site to pay respects or participate in a ritual at the site, the act of travel is called a ___________.
42. ___________ _______ are places or spaces people infuse with religious meaning.
43. The ancient city of Jerusalem is sacred to ______, __________, and ________.
44. The most important sacred site for Jews is the __________ _______ (also called the Wailing Wall), at the edge of the Temple Mount in Jerusalem (Figure 7.20). The Temple Mount occupies the top of a modest hill where, according to the Torah, Abraham almost sacrificed his son ________.
45. For Christians, Jerusalem is sacred both because of the sacrifice Abraham was willing to make of his son at the ___________ _______ and because Jesus' crucifixion took place just outside of the city's walls. Jesus was then buried in a tomb that Roman Emperor Constantine later marked with a basilica that is now the Church of the _______ ___________.
46. Muslims constructed a mosque called the _______ of the Rock adjacent to the Western Wall to mark the site where Muslims believe Muhammad arrived from Mecca and then ascended into heaven (Figure 7.20). The site Jews call _______ ___________ is called al-Haram al-Sharif (the Noble Sanctuary) by Muslims.
47. Hindus believe that the erection of a _______, whether modest or elaborate, bestows merit on the builder and will be rewarded. As a result, the Hindu cultural landscape—urban as well as rural—is dotted with countless ________, ranging from small village temples to structures so large and elaborate that they are virtually holy cities.
48. When Buddha received enlightenment, he sat under a large tree, the ________ (enlightenment) tree at Bodh Gaya in India.

49. The _________ ________________ of Christianity's branches reflect the changes the faith has undergone over the centuries. In medieval Europe the _________, church, or monastery was the focus of life.

50. The New England region is strongly _________; the South's leading denomination is ________; the Upper Midwest has large numbers of _________; and the Southwest is predominantly Spanish Catholic.

52. Elaborate, sometimes magnificently designed mosques whose balconied ___________ rise above the townscape dominate Islamic cities, towns, and villages.

53. One of the best-known pilgrimages in the modern world is the Muslim pilgrimage to Mecca, the ______.

WHAT ROLE DOES RELIGION PLAY IN POLITICAL CONFLICTS?

54. A comparison between Figure 7.6 and a political map of the world reveals that some countries lie entirely within the realms of individual world religions, whereas other countries straddle __________ boundaries, the boundaries ___________ the world's major faiths.

55. Other countries with major religious disputes straddle __________ boundaries, the boundaries _________ a single major faith. Intrafaith boundaries include divisions between Christian _____________ and Catholics (Northern Ireland), divisions between Muslim Sunni and Shi'ite (Iraq), and the like.

56. The situation in _________ and Palestine today does not reflect a simple interfaith boundary.

57. Like other countries in West Africa, Nigeria is predominantly _________ in the north, and _______________ and animist in the south. With over 168 million people, Nigeria is Africa's most populous country.

58. Since 2009, the worst violence in Nigeria has taken place in the northern half of the country, along the interfaith boundary and in the northeast where the extremist Muslim group, ________ ________, operates.

59. The drive toward religious ____________ is often born out of frustration over the perceived ____________ of society's morals and values, lack of religious authority, failure to achieve economic goals, loss of a sense of local control, failure of a government to protect a religion, or a sense of violation of a religion's core territory.

60. Religious ___________ is fundamentalism carried to the point of ___________.

61. Like all other major religions, Judaism has __________ sects. The most conservative of the three major sects of Judaism is ___________.

62. Judaism also has its _________ element—people whom the majority of Jews denounce and whom the government of Israel has even banned from the country. Among the Jewish extremist groups is the Kach and __________ ______—followers of the late American-born, Israeli Rabbi Meir Kahane.

63. The _________ in Afghanistan also provided a haven for the activities of Islamic extremists who sought to promote an Islamic holy war, or _______, against the West in general and the United States in particular.

Step 4: "Map It" Quiz: Use the maps from the text to answer the questions.

1. What religion dominates South America (Figure 7.6)?
   A. Protestant
   B. Islam
   C. Indigenous Religions
   D. Roman Catholic
   E. Eastern Orthodox

2. What religion dominates North Africa and Southwest Asia (Figure 7.6)?
   A. Protestant
   B. Islam
   C. indigenous religions
   D. Eastern Orthodox
   E. Roman Catholic

3. Hinduism and Shintoism are ethnic religions that concentrate in these two countries, respectively (Figure 7.6):
   A. Pakistan and China
   B. Pakistan and Japan
   C. India and South Korea
   D. India and Japan
   E. Bangladesh and the Philippines

4. Which two religions are correctly paired in the Western hearth (Figure 7.9)?
   A. Islam and Hinduism
   B. Buddhism and Christianity
   C. Islam and Christianity
   D. Hinduism and Buddhism
   E. Buddhism and Islam

5. According to Figure 7.16, how did Islam get to Indonesia?
   A. It originated there.
   B. through conquest
   C. through trade
   D. through relocation diffusion
   E. Islam never got to Indonesia.

Step 5: AP-Style Practice Quiz

1. The ideology of Zionism has as its goal:
   A. the merger of Judaism with other religions
   B. the merger of the three modern divisions of Judaism
   C. a homeland for the Jewish people
   D. the elimination of the Orthodox division within the faith
   E. the search for the true Mount Zion where the Ten Commandments were revealed

2. The youngest major religion is:
   A. Hinduism
   B. Judaism
   C. Islam
   D. Christianity
   E. Buddhism

3. Modern-day Shi'a Islam dominates a region centered on:
   A. Pakistan and Afghanistan
   B. Saudi Arabia and Oman
   C. Armenia and Azerbaijan
   D. Indonesia and Malaysia
   E. Iran and Iraq

4. The Hajj, one of the "pillars of Islam," is:
   A. charitable giving
   B. fasting during the holy month
   C. the veil worn by Muslim women
   D. the pilgrimage to Mecca
   E. the five daily prayers

5. The world's largest Islamic state with regard to population is:
   A. Iran
   B. Pakistan
   C. Egypt
   D. Indonesia
   E. India

6. The Jews of Central Europe are known as:
   A. Ashkenazim
   B. Sephardim
   C. Zionists
   D. Orthodox
   E. Reformed

7. The faith that is most widely dispersed over the world is:
   A. Christianity
   B. Islam
   C. Shamanism
   D. Buddhism
   E. Baha'i Faith

8. Sikhism is a small compromise religion that arose from the confrontation between Hinduism and:
   A. Buddhism
   B. Jainism
   C. Christianity
   D. British colonial officials
   E. Islam

9. Zoroastrianism is similar to Islam and Christianity in that it is:
   A. a world religion
   B. monotheistic
   C. a missionary religion
   D. polytheistic
   E. a desert faith in origin

10. The diaspora of the Jews resulted from:
   A. Moses' decision to leave Egypt
   B. the Arab-Israeli conflict
   C. the holocaust
   D. the Roman destruction of Jerusalem
   E. disagreements between the Sadducees and the Pharisees

CHAPTER 8:
POLITICAL GEOGRAPHY

Name: Sanya B. ______ Period ______ Date ______
Chapter Title: ______
Chapter # ______ Pgs. ______ to ______

The Five Steps to Chapter Success

Step 1: Read the Chapter Summary below and preview the Key Questions.
Step 2: Complete the Pre-Reading Activity (PRA) for this chapter.
Step 3: Read the chapter and complete the guided worksheet.
Step 4: Read the maps and take the "Map It!"quiz
Step 5: Take an AP-style Practice Quiz

STEP 1: Chapter Summary and Key Questions

Chapter Summary

We tend to take the state for granted, but the modern state idea is less than 400 years old. The idea and ideal of the nation-state have diffused around the globe in the wake of colonialism and the emergence of the modern international legal order.

The state may seem natural and permanent, but it is not. New states are being recognized, and existing states are vulnerable to destructive forces. How long can this way of politically organizing space last?

As we look to arrangements beyond the state, we can turn to the global scale and consider what places the global world economy most affects, shapes, and benefits. In the next chapter, we study global cities with major links in the world economy. Global cities dominate their surroundings and connect with each other across the world in many ways that transcend the state.

Key Questions

Field Note: Challenging the Political-Territorial Order	p. 211–213
1. How is space politically organized into states and nations?	p. 213–222
2. How do states spatially organize their governments?	p. 222–230
3. How are boundaries established, and why do boundary disputes occur?	p. 230–234
4. How does the study of geopolitics help us understand the world?	p. 234–237
5. What are supranational organizations, and what is the future of the state?	p. 237–243

Step 2: Pre-Reading Activity (PRA)

1. Write down each of the Key Questions with the fewest pages and the most pages.

Key Question	# of Pages
How does the study of geopolitics help us understand the world?	3
How is space politically organized into states and nations?	9

2. After looking over the Key Questions and the Chapter Summary, write a few sentences about what you expect to learn in general in this chapter.

In this unit, I expect to learn about the study of politics among geographers. Furthermore, I will learn about the ways of division within a nation.

3. How many world maps are there in this chapter? 15 (Go to Student Companion Website and print out organizers for help.)

4. Read the Field Note introduction of the chapter and list five specific facts you learned.

- Decolonization was fueled by desire for political and economic independence
- 1648, west Europe exerted control over populations
- States represent people AND organized militaries
- Economic independence = impossible
- political activity is engaged in by EVERYONE

5. Go to Step 1 and look at the Geographic Concepts. Create a list of terms you think you know and terms you need to know.

I THINK I KNOW	I NEED TO LEARN
state	Mercantilism
sovereignty	commodification
nation	centrifugal
colonialism	devolution

Step 3: Chapter 8 Guided Worksheet

Directions: As you read the chapter, fill in the blanks on the guided worksheet.

FIELD NOTE—CHALLENGING THE POLITICAL-TERRITORIAL ORDER

1. For more than a decade, Europe's common currency has been a visible representation of a project that has reshaped the political map of the continent. The states of the EU have pooled key aspects of their sovereignty, creating a new political-territorial unit that has become an increasingly significant actor in local and global affairs.
2. The rise of the EU and the adoption of a common currency represent efforts to create a political and economic unit at a different scale—one that its proponents hope can be a more influential global actor than any individual country could be and that can produce economic and social advantages within its borders.

HOW IS SPACE POLITICALLY ORGANIZED INTO STATES AND NATIONS?

3. Political geography is the study of the political organization of the world.
4. A state is a politically organized territory with a permanent population, a defined territory, and a government. To be a state, an entity must be recognized as such by other states.
5. Today, territoriality is tied to the concept of sovereignty. Sovereignty refers to a government's right to control its own territory, both politically and militarily.
6. The event in European history that marks the formal beginning of the modern state system is the Peace of Westphalia, negotiated in 1648 among the princes of the states making up the Holy Roman Empire, as well as a few neighboring states.
7. The popular media and press often use the words "nation," "state," and "country" interchangeably. Political geographers use state and country interchangeably (often preferring state), but the word "nation" is distinct.
8. The aforementioned ambiguity reflects the fact that a nation was traditionally understood to be a group of people who think of themselves as one based on a sense of shared culture and history, and who seek some degree of political-territorial autonomy.
9. A nation-state is a politically organized area in which nation and state occupy the same space. Since few (if any) states are nation-states, the importance of the concept of the nation-state lies primarily in the idea behind it.
10. Nearly every state in the world is a multinational state, a state with more than one nation inside its borders. The people living in the former state of Yugoslavia never achieved a strong sense of Yugoslav nationhood.
11. When a nation stretches across borders and across states, the nation is called a multistate nation. Political geographer George White studied the states of Romania and Hungary and their overlapping nations
12. Another complication that arises from the lack of fit between nations and states is that some nations do not have a state; they are stateless nations. The Palestinians are an example of a stateless nation.

13. A much larger stateless nation is the Kurds, a group comprising 25 to 30 million people living in an area called Kurdistan that covers parts of 6 states.
14. Europe exported its concepts of state, sovereignty, and the desire for nation-states to much of the rest of the world through two waves of colonialism.
15. During the heyday of colonialism, the imperial powers exercised ruthless control over their domains and organized them for maximum economic exploitation. Colonizers organized the flows of raw materials for their own benefit.
16. The long-term impacts of colonialism are many and varied. Of course, not all Europeans profited equally from colonialism. Enormous poverty persisted within even the most powerful European states.
17. Building on the work of Immanuel Wallerstein, proponents of world-systems theory view the world as much more than the sum total of the world's states.
18. Capitalism means that in the world-economy, individuals, corporations, and states own land and produce goods and services that are exchanged for profit.
19. Lastly, world-systems theorists see the world-economy as a three-tiered structure comprised of a core, a periphery, and a semiperiphery.
20. The core and the periphery are not just places but the sites where particular processes take place. The core is where one is most likely to find higher levels of education, higher salaries, and more technology—core processes that generate more wealth in the world-economy. The periphery more commonly has lower levels of education, lower salaries, and less sophisticated technology—peripheral processes associated with a more marginal position in the world-economy.
21. The map designates some states as part of the semiperiphery—places where core and periphery processes are both occurring—places that are exploited by the core but in turn exploit the periphery.

HOW DO STATES SPATIALLY ORGANIZE THEIR GOVERNMENTS?

22. In the 1950s, political geographer Richard Hartshorne described the forces within the state that unify the people as centripetal and the forces that divide them as centrifugal.
23. The internal political geographic organization of states can have an impact on state unity. Most states in the world are either unitary or federal states.
24. Until the end of World War II, many European states, including multinational states, were highly centralized, with the capital city serving as the focus of power. Political geographers call these highly centralized states unitary governments.
25. One way of governing a multinational state is to construct a federal system, organizing state territory into regions, substates (which we refer to as States), provinces, or cantons.
26. In Nigeria, the 36 constituent States choose their own judicial system. In the Muslim north, 12 States have Shari'a laws (legal systems based on traditional Islamic laws), and in the Christian and animist south, the States do not.
27. Devolution is the movement of power "downward" from the central government to regional governments within the state.

28. Many of Europe's devolutionary movements came from nations within a state that define themselves as being ethnically, linguistically, or religiously distinct. In the case of Czechoslovakia, the process was peaceful: Czechs and Slovaks divided their country, creating a new international border in 1992.
29. Devolutionary pressures often arise from a combination of sources. In Catalonia, ethnocultural differences play a significant role, but economics plays a role as well; with some 8 percent of Spain's territory and just 16 percent of its population, Catalonia produces some 35 percent of all Spanish exports by value and 54 percent of its high-tech exports.
31. Electoral geographers examine how the spatial configuration of electoral districts and the voting patterns that emerge in particular elections reflect and influence social and political affairs.
32. The United States Constitution establishes a system of territorial representation. In the Senate, each major territorial unit (State) gets two representatives, and the 435 members of the House of Representatives are elected from territorially defined districts that have similar-sized populations.
33. Reapportionment is the process by which districts are moved according to population shifts, so that each district encompasses approximately the same number of people.
34. Strange-looking districts constructed to attain certain political ends are nothing new in American politics. In 1812, Governor Elbridge Gerry of Massachusetts signed into law a district designed to give an advantage to his party—a district that looked so odd to artist Gilbert Stuart that he drew it with a head, wings, and claws. Stuart called it the "salamander district," but a colleague immortalized it by naming it a gerrymander (after the governor). Ever since, the term *gerrymandering* has been used to describe "redistricting for advantage."

HOW ARE BOUNDARIES ESTABLISHED, AND WHY DO BOUNDARY DISPUTES OCCUR?

35. A boundary between states is actually a vertical plane that cuts through the rocks below (called the subsoil) and the airspace above, dividing one state from another.
36. Above the ground, too, the interpretation of boundaries as vertical planes has serious implications. A state's "airspace" is defined by the atmosphere above its land area as marked by its boundaries, as well as by what lies beyond, at higher altitudes.
37. When boundaries are drawn using grid systems such as latitude and longitude or township and range, political geographers refer to these boundaries as geometric boundaries.
38. Physical-political boundaries (also called natural-political boundaries) are boundaries that follow an agreed-upon feature in the natural landscape, such as the center point of a river or the crest of a mountain range. The Rio Grande is an important physical-political boundary between the United States and Mexico.
39. Definitional boundary disputes focus on the legal language of the boundary agreement. For example, a boundary definition may stipulate that the median line of a river will mark the boundary.
40. Locational boundary disputes center on the delimitation and possibly the demarcation of the boundary.

41. Operational boundary disputes involve neighboring states that differ over the way their border should function. When two adjoining countries agree on how cross-border migration should be controlled, the border functions satisfactorily.

42. Allocational boundary disputes of the kind described earlier, involving the Netherlands and Germany over natural gas and Iraq and Kuwait over oil, are becoming more common as the search for resources intensifies.

HOW DOES THE STUDY OF GEOPOLITICS HELP US UNDERSTAND THE WORLD?

43. Geopoliticians of the time generally fit into one of two camps: the German school, which sought to explain why and how certain states became powerful, and the British/American school, which sought to offer strategic advice by identifying parts of Earth's surface that were particularly important for the maintenance and projection of power.

44. The first political geographer who studied these issues was the German professor Friedrich Ratzel. His ideas were so speculative that it might have been forgotten if some of Ratzel's German followers in the 1930s had not translated his abstract writings into policy recommendations that ultimately were used to justify Nazi expansionism.

45. To many of his contemporaries the oceans—the paths to colonies and trade—were the key to world domination, but Mackinder disagreed. He concluded that a land based power, not a sea power, would ultimately rule the world. At the heart of Eurasia, he argued, lay an impregnable, resource-rich "pivot area" extending from eastern Europe to eastern Siberia.

46. When Mackinder proposed his heartland theory, there was little to foretell the rise of a superpower in the heartland.

47. When geopolitical strategists and intellectuals of statecraft predict future geopolitical orders, they often assume that individual states will continue to be the dominant actors in the international arena. The rise of regional blocs could alter the system, with key clusters of states functioning as major geopolitical nodes.

WHAT ARE SUPRANATIONAL ORGANIZATIONS, AND WHAT IS THE FUTURE OF THE STATE?

48. A supranational organization is an entity composed of three or more states that forges an association and forms an administrative structure for mutual benefit and in pursuit of shared goals.

49. The modern beginnings of the supranational movement can be traced to conferences following World War I.

50. After World War II, a new organization was founded in an effort to promote international security and cooperation: the United Nations.

51. From the European states' involvement in the Marshall Plan came the Organization for European Economic Cooperation (OEEC), a body that in turn gave rise to other cooperative organizations.

52. In the late 1990s, the EU began preparing for the establishment of a single currency—the euro. First, all electronic financial transactions were denominated in euros, and on January 1, 2002, the EU introduced euro coins and notes. Not all EU member states are currently a part of the euro zone, but the euro has emerged as a significant global currency.

53. Supranationalism is a worldwide phenomenon. Other economic associations, such as the North American Free Trade Agreement (NAFTA), the Association of Caribbean States (ACS), the Central American Common Market, the Andean Group, the Southern Cone Community Market (MERCOSUR), the Economic Community of West African States (ECOWAS), the Asia-Pacific Economic Council (APEC), and the Commonwealth of Independent States (CIS), have drawn up treaties to reduce tariffs and import restrictions in order to ease the flow of commerce in their regions.

54. Yet, when we turn back to the European Union, we see a supranational organization that is unlike any other.

Step 4: "Map It" Quiz: Use the maps from the text to answer the questions.

1. Which of the following regions had most of the countries that became independent after 1940 (Figure 8.2)?
   A. North America
   B. South America
   C. South Asia
   D. East Asia
   E. Austral

2. Which of the following is still a colony (Figure 8.2)?
   A. Cuba
   B. Greenland
   C. India
   D. Namibia
   E. Kazakhstan

3. What colonial power dominated Northwest Africa (Figure 8.7)?
   A. Great Britain
   B. France
   C. Germany
   D. Portugal
   E. Spain

4. Which of the following non-European countries had colonies (Figure 8.7)?
   A. Australia
   B. Indonesia
   C. Saudi Arabia
   D. South Korea
   E. Japan

5. Which of the following countries is in the periphery (Figure 8.9)?
   A. China
   B. South Korea
   C. Mongolia
   D. Japan
   E. India

Step 5: AP-Style Practice Quiz

1. The United Nations is not a world government, but in recent years individual states have asked the UN to do a number of different things, the primary goal of which is:
   A. creating a common global currency
   B. monitoring elections
   C. providing for refugees
   D. setting maritime boundaries
   E. fostering international security and cooperation

2. The European Union's future expansion into the Muslim realm by the inclusion of ________ is highly controversial and strongly opposed by Greece.
   A. Saudi Arabia
   B. Bosnia
   C. Algeria
   D. Turkey
   E. Iraq

3. Sir Halford Mackinder developed what would become known as the heartland theory, which suggested that interior Eurasia contained a critical "pivot area" that would generate a state capable of world domination. The key to the area according to Mackinder was:
   A. natural protection
   B. distance
   C. natural resources
   D. western Europe
   E. naval power

4. The movement of power from the central government to regional governments is referred to as:
   A. revolution
   B. pluralism
   C. supranationalism
   D. devolution
   E. decentralization

5. The boundaries of independent African states were drawn at the Berlin Conference and were essentially drawn along ________ lines.
   A. arbitrary
   B. ethnic
   C. religious
   D. ecological
   E. linguistic

6. Yugoslavia was a prime example of a:
   A. multistate nation
   B. nation-state
   C. stateless nation
   D. unitary state
   E. multinational state

7. The present number of countries and territories in the world is approximately:
   A. 400
   B. 350
   C. 300
   D. 200
   E. 100

8. The view of human territorial behavior implies an expression of control over space and time. This control is closely related to the concept of:
   A. nationhood
   B. colonialism
   C. sovereignty
   D. warfare
   E. hegemony

9. Nigeria is a state with a federal system of government. This fact is reflected in the adoption of ________ law in the states of the Muslim North.
   A. British Common
   B. Nigerian Federal
   C. Sharia
   D. local tribal
   E. states' rights

10. Listed among the challenges to the state in the twenty-first century are all the following EXCEPT:
   A. nuclear weapons
   B. economic globalization
   C. increased cultural communication
   D. terrorism in the name of religion
   E. the United Nations

245-259

CHAPTER 9:
URBAN GEOGRAPHY

Name: ______________________________ **Period** __________ **Date** __________

Chapter Title: ____

Chapter # ______________________________ **Pgs.** __________ **to** __________

The Five Steps to Chapter Success

Step 1: Read the Chapter Summary below and preview the Key Questions.

Step 2: Complete the Pre-Reading Activity (PRA) for this chapter.

Step 3: Read the chapter and complete the guided worksheet.

Step 4: Read the maps and take the "Map It!"quiz

Step 5: Take an AP-style Practice Quiz

STEP 1: Chapter Summary and Key Questions

Chapter Summary

The city is an ever changing cultural landscape, its layers reflecting grand plans by governments, impassioned pursuits by individuals, economic decisions by corporations, and processes of globalization. Geographers who study cities have a multitude of topics to examine. From gentrification to tear-downs, from favelas to McMansions, from spaces of production to spaces of consumption, from ancient walls to gated communities, cities have so much in common and yet each has its own pulse, its own feel, its own spatial structure, its own set of realities. The pulse of the city is undoubtedly created by the peoples and cultures who live there. For it is the people, whether working independently or as part of global institutions, who continuously create and re-create the city and its geography.

Key Questions

Field Note: Ghosts of Detroit?	p. 245–247
1. When and why did people start living in cities?	p. 247–259
2. Where are cities located and why?	p. 259–261
3. How are cities organized, and how do they function?	p. 261–268
4. How do people shape cities?	p. 269–282
5. What role do cities play in globalization?	p. 283–286

Step 2: Pre-Reading Activity (PRA)

1. Write down each of the Key Questions with the fewest pages and the most pages.

Key Question	# of Pages
Where are cities organized, and how do they function?	2
Why and when did people start living in cities?	12

2. After looking over the Key Questions and the Chapter Summary, write a few sentences about what you expect to learn in general in this chapter.

In general, I expect to learn about how cities are organized and why they are organized that way. Furthermore, I will learn about how civilizations shape cities.

3. How many world maps are there in this chapter? 3 (Go to Student Companion Website and print out organizers for help.)

4. Read the Field Note introduction of the chapter and list five specific facts you learned.

- Grand Circus Park in Detroit is a central business district
- Downtown Detroit Development Authority requires investors to save the façade of the building
- people are drawn to living downtown because of high gas price and low crime rates
- abandoned high rise buildings = Ghosts of Detroit

5. Go to Step 1 and look at the Geographic Concepts. Create a list of terms you think you know and terms you need to know.

I THINK I KNOW	I NEED TO LEARN
gated communities	spaces of consumption
zoning laws	informal economy
megacities	urbicide
suburbanization	urban sprawl

Step 3: Chapter 9 Guided Worksheet

Directions: As you read the chapter, fill in the blanks on the guided worksheet.

FIELD NOTE—GHOSTS OF DETROIT

1. The grouping of buildings along Grand Circus Park reflects the rise, fall, and revitalization of the central business district (CBD) in Detroit. The central business district is a concentration of businesses and commerce in the city's downtown.
2. Other neighborhoods of the city are not bouncing back as well. Abandoned high-rise buildings called the ghosts of Detroit are joined by empty single-family homes. The population of Detroit rose and fell with the automobile industry. The population peaked at 1.8 million in 1950, but a 2014 U.S. Census Bureau report estimates the city's population falling to below 700,000.
3. Geographers are leading the study of cities today, focusing on the impacts of developments at different scales on cities, including the ways in which globalization and political-economic shifts are affecting the organization and character of urban areas.

WHEN AND WHY DID PEOPLE START LIVING IN CITIES

4. Worldwide, more people live in urban areas than in rural areas today. Urban refers to the built-up space of the central city and suburbs.
5. A city is an agglomeration of people and businesses clustered together to serve as a center of politics, culture, and economics.
6. Archaeologists, anthropologists, and geographers have studied the remains and records of the first cities, creating numerous theories as to how cities came about. Most agree that some series of events led to the formation of an agricultural surplus and a leadership class; which came first varies by theory.
7. The innovation of the city is called the first urban revolution, and it occurred independently in six separate hearths, a case of independent invention.
8. This urban hearth is called Mesopotamia, referring to the region of great cities (such as Ur and Babylon) located between the Tigris and Euphrates rivers. The second hearth of urbanization, in the Nile River Valley, dates back to 3200 BCE. The third urban hearth, dating to 2200 BCE, is the Indus River Valley, another place where agriculture likely diffused from the Fertile Crescent.
9. The fourth urban hearth arose around the confluence of the Huang He (Yellow) and Wei Valleys of present-day China, dating to 1500 BCE. Chronologically, the fifth urban hearth, found in Mesoamerica, dates to 1100 BCE. The ancient cities of Mesoamerica were religious centers. The most recent archaeological evidence establishes Peru as the sixth urban hearth chronologically.
10. The cities of Mesopotamia and the Nile Valley may have had between 10,000 and 15,000 inhabitants after nearly 2000 years of growth and development.

11. Greece is more accurately described as a secondary hearth of urbanization because the Greek city influenced urban developments in Europe and beyond, as European ideas diffused around the world during the colonial era. Every city had its acropolis (acro meaning high point; polis meaning city), on which the people built the most impressive structures—usually religious buildings.
12. As time went on, this public space, called the agora (meaning market), also became the focus of commercial activity. The site of a city is its absolute location, often chosen for its advantages in trade or defense, or as a center for religious practice. The situation of a city refers to its position in relation to the surrounding context.
13. The Romans were greatly influenced by the Greeks, as is evident in Roman mythology and visible in the cultural landscape and urban morphology of Roman cities. The Romans took the Greek acropolis (zone of religion and center of power) and agora (zone of public space and the marketplace) and combined them into one zone: the Forum, which served as the focal point of Roman public life.
14. Coastal cities remained crucial after exploration led to colonialism. During the colonial period, key cities in international trade networks included the coastal cities of Cape Town (South Africa), Lima-Callao (Peru), and New York City.
15. Before the second urban revolution could take place, a second revolution in agriculture was necessary. During the late seventeenth century and into the eighteenth century, Europeans made a series of important improvements in agriculture, including invention of the seed drill, hybrid seeds, and improved breeding practices for livestock.
16. Living conditions were dreadful for workers in cities, and working conditions were shocking. Children worked 12-hour shifts in textile mills, typically 6 days a week.

WHERE ARE CITIES LOCATED AND WHY?

17. Site and situation help explain why certain cities were planned and why cities thrive or fail.
18. In studying the size of cities and distances between them, urban geographers explored the trade areas of different-size cities. Customers from smaller towns and villages come to the city to shop and to conduct other business.
19. The rank-size rule holds that in a model urban hierarchy, the population of a city or town will be inversely proportional to its rank in the hierarchy. Thus, if the largest city has 12 million people, the second largest will have about 6 million (that is, half the population of the largest city); the third city will have 4 million (one-third); the fourth city 3 million; and so on.
20. In 1939, geographer Mark Jefferson defined a primate city as "a country's leading city, always disproportionately large and exceptionally expressive of national capacity and feeling." He saw the primate city as the largest and most economically influential within the state, with the next largest city in the state being much smaller and much less influential.
21. In his book *The Central Places in Southern Germany* (1933), Christaller laid the groundwork for central place theory. His goal was to predict where central places in the urban hierarchy (hamlets, villages, towns, and cities) would be located.

22. Urban geographers were divided on the relevance of his model. Some saw hexagonal systems everywhere; others saw none at all.

HOW ARE CITIES ORGANIZED AND HOW DO THEY FUNCTION?

23. One way to conceptualize the layout of cities is through models that illustrate the structures of cities.
24. Each model of the city, regardless of the region, is a study in functional zonation—the division of the city into certain regions (zones) for certain purposes (functions).
25. Suburbanization is the process by which lands that were previously outside of the urban environment become urbanized, as people and businesses from the city move to these spaces.
26. Following World War II, the availability of personal automobiles and the construction of ring roads and other arteries around cities led to rapid suburbanization, especially around new transportation corridors.
27. Suburban downtowns emerged to serve their new local economies. Often located near key freeway intersections, these suburban downtowns developed mainly around big regional shopping centers and attracted industrial parks, office complexes, hotels, restaurants, entertainment facilities, and even sports stadiums.
28. Present-day Los Angeles and Toronto are cited as prime examples of what is sometimes called a galactic city—a complex urban area in which centrality of functions is no longer significant.
29. The rapid growth in the population and territorial footprint of megacities in the developing world has made it difficult to model many urban areas.
30. In 1980, geographers Ernst Griffin and Larry Ford studied South American cities and derived a model of the South American city referred to as the Griffin–Ford model.
31. Shantytowns are unplanned developments of crude dwellings and shelters made mostly of scrap wood, iron, and pieces of cardboard that develop around cities.
32. A structural element common to many South American cities is the disamenity sector, the very poorest parts of cities that in extreme cases are not connected to regular city services and are controlled by gangs and drug lords.
33. The imprint of European colonialism can still be seen in many African cities.
34. As a result of this diversity, it is difficult to formulate a model of the African city. Studies of African cities indicate that the central city often consists of not one but 3 CBDs (Figure 9.25): a remnant of the colonial CBD, an informal and sometimes periodic market zone, and a transitional business center where commerce is conducted from curbside, stalls, or storefronts.
35. Some of the most populated cities in the world are in Southeast Asia. The city of Kuala Lumpur, Malaysia, is a complex of high-rise development, including the 1483-foot-tall Petronas Towers, which until recently was the world's tallest building.
36. In 1967, urban geographer T. G. McGee studied the medium-sized cities of Southeast Asia and found that they exhibit similar land-use patterns, creating a model referred to as the McGee model.

HOW DO PEOPLE SHAPE CITIES?

37. Government planning agencies can directly affect the layout of cities by restricting the kinds of development allowed in certain regions or zones of cities. Through zoning laws, cities divide up the city and designate the kinds of development allowed in each zone.
38. Portland, Oregon, is often described as the best planned city in North America because it is built around free transportation in the central city to discourage the use of cars. On the other hand, Houston, Texas, is the only large city that does not have zoning laws on the books.
39. Many of the world's most populous cities are located in the less prosperous parts of the world, including São Paulo (Brazil), Mexico City (Mexico), Mumbai (India), Dhaka (Bangladesh), and Dehli (India).
40. Cities in poorer parts of the world generally lack enforceable zoning laws. Without zoning laws, cities in the periphery have mixed land use throughout the city.
41. Across the global periphery, the one trait all major cities display is the stark contrast between the wealthy and the poor.
42. For example, before the civil rights movement of the 1960s, financial institutions in the business of lending money could engage in a practice known as redlining.
43. In a practice called blockbusting, realtors would solicit white residents of the neighborhood to sell their homes under the guise that the neighborhood was going downhill because a black person or family had moved in. This produced what urban geographers and sociologists call white flight—movement of whites from the city and adjacent neighborhoods to the outlying suburbs.
44. A process called gentrification—the rehabilitation of deteriorated houses in low-income neighborhoods—took hold in areas near the centers of many cities.
45. The homes intended for suburban demolition are called teardowns. In their place, suburbanites build newer homes that often are supersized and stretch to the outer limits of the lot. New supersized mansions are sometimes called McMansions.
46. As populations have grown in certain areas of the United States, such as the Sun Belt and the West, urban areas have experienced urban sprawl—unrestricted growth of housing, commercial developments, and roads over large expanses of land, with little concern for urban planning.
47. Although some see new urbanist designs as manufactured communities and feel disconnected in a new urbanist space, others see these designs as an important antidote to sprawl.
48. Gated communities are fenced-in neighborhoods with controlled access gates for people and automobiles. Often, gated communities have security cameras and security forces (privatized police) keeping watch over the community, as the main objective of a gated community is to create a space of safety within the uncertain urban world.
49. What prevails here is referred to as the informal economy—the economy that is not taxed and is not counted toward a country's gross national income.

50. Even as the informal economy thrives among the millions in the shantytowns, the new era of globalization is making a major impact in the larger cities founded or fostered by the colonial powers.

WHAT ROLE DO CITIES PLAY IN GLOBALIZATION?

51. World cities function at the global scale, beyond the reach of the state borders, functioning as the service centers of the world economy.
52. In addition to being nodes in globalization, cities are also products of globalization.

Step 4: "Map It" Quiz: Use the maps from the text to answer the questions.

1. Which of the following regions had the largest number of countries with urbanization lower than 39 percent and below?
   A. Southeast Asia
   B. South Asia
   C. East Asia
   D. Subsaharan Africa
   E. South America

2. Which of the following countries is not 70 percent or above in urban population?
   A. Egypt
   B. Brazil
   C. South Africa
   D. Russia
   E. Turkey

3. Which of the following regions was NOT a hearth of urbanization?
   A. North Africa and Southwest Asia
   B. Middle America
   C. South Asia
   D. Europe
   E. East Asia

4. Which of the following is NOT an alpha world city?
   A. Chicago
   B. Tokyo
   C. Paris
   D. São Paulo
   E. Seattle

Step 5: AP-Style Practice Quiz

1. Segregation in the United States was reinforced by the financial practice known as:
   A. redlining
   B. community block grants
   C. land-use zoning
   D. tax-increment financing
   E. microcredit

2. In core-area cities, the practice of buying up and rehabilitating deteriorating housing, which resulted in raising housing values and a social change in neighborhoods, is called:
   A. public housing
   B. gentrification
   C. white flight
   D. urban renewal
   E. revitalization

3. The huge influx of population from rural to urban areas in peripheral or semiperipheral areas (less developed countries) finds housing in:
   A. public housing
   B. edge cities
   C. deteriorating CBDs
   D. high-density apartments
   E. shantytowns

4. Which of the following is the most rapidly urbanizing realm of the world?
   A. Middle America
   B. Africa south of the Sahara
   C. East Asia
   D. South Asia
   E. the Middle East

5. The relative location of a city refers to its:
   A. site
   B. situation
   C. genealogy of development
   D. approximate latitude and longitude
   E. physical characteristics

6. The manufacturing city (post-Industrial Revolution) first emerged in:
   A. the British Midlands
   B. central Italy
   C. the French coastal region
   D. the Ruhr
   E. Appalachia

7. In which of the following regions did urbanization develop first?
   A. Mesopotamia
   B. Nile River Valley
   C. Indus River Valley
   D. China
   E. Mesoamerica

8. The layout of a city, the physical form and structure, is referred to as:
   A. zoning
   B. urban grid
   C. city plan
   D. urban street pattern
   E. urban morphology

9. A hinterland reveals the _______ of each settlement.
   A. total population
   B. working population
   C. economic reach
   D. aggregate purchasing power
   E. quality of agricultural land

10. Paris and Mexico City are many times larger than the second-ranked city in their respective countries. Their disproportionate size illustrates:
    A. the concept of the primate city
    B. the fact that capital cities are always very large
    C. the rank-size rule
    D. the effects of suburbanization
    E. urban power structures

CHAPTER 10:
DEVELOPMENT

Name: ______________________________ **Period** __________ **Date** ____________

Chapter Title: ____

Chapter # ______________________________ **Pgs.** ____________ **to** ____________

The Five Steps to Chapter Success

Step 1: Read the Chapter Summary below and preview the Key Questions.
Step 2: Complete the Pre-Reading Activity (PRA) for this chapter.
Step 3: Read the chapter and complete the guided worksheet.
Step 4: Read the maps and take the "Map It!"quiz
Step 5: Take an AP-style Practice Quiz

STEP 1: Chapter Summary and Key Questions

Chapter Summary

The idea of economic development is relatively new; it implies a sense of progressively improving a country's economic situation. The idea took hold in the wake of the Industrial Revolution. Geographers focus on the spatial structure of the economy, assessing how that structure influences the ability of states and regions to reach greater levels of economic development. Geographers also recognize that economic development in a single place is based on a multitude of factors, including the situation within the global economy, the link the place plays in commodity chains, the efficacy of government, the presence of disease, the health and well-being of the population, the presence and amount of foreign debt, the success or failure of government policies, and the influence of nongovernmental programs. Geographers also realize that all of these processes are operating concurrently across scales, making a country's journey toward economic development much more complicated than climbing a ladder.

Key Questions

Field Note: Geography, Trade, and Development	p. 288–289
1. How is development defined and measured?	p. 289–296
2. How does geographical context affect development??	p. 296–298
3. What are the barriers to and the costs of economic development?	p. 298–305
4. How do political and economic institutions influence uneven development within states?	p. 305–310

Step 2: Pre-Reading Activity (PRA)

1. Write down each of the Key Questions with the fewest pages and the most pages.

Key Question	# of Pages
How does geographical context affect development?	2
How is development defined and measured	7

2. After looking over the Key Questions and the Chapter Summary, write a few sentences about what you expect to learn in general in this chapter.

In general, I expect to learn the key distinctions between developed and developing regions. Furthermore, I want to know what factors label a region as developed or underdeveloped

3. How many world maps are there in this chapter? 6 (Go to Student Companion Website and print out organizers for help.)

4. Read the Field Note introduction of the chapter and list three specific facts you learned.

- commodity chain = links that connect places of production and distribution

- Timbuktu was a break-of-bulk location

- Timbuktu declined due to shifted trade patterns

5. Go to Step 1 and look at the Geographic Concepts. Create a list of terms you think you know and terms you need to know.

I THINK I KNOW	I NEED TO LEARN
GDP (gross domestic product)	GNI (gross national income)
modernization model	digital divide
world-system's theory	neoliberalism
three-tier structure	EPZ

Step 3: Chapter 10 Guided Worksheet

Directions: As you read the chapter, fill in the blanks on the guided worksheet.

FIELD NOTE—GEOGRAPHY, TRADE, AND DEVELOPMENT

1. Timbuktu's story serves as a reminder that where a place is ____________ in relation to patterns of economic development and exchange can be as ______________ as, or even more important than, the commodities found in that place.
2. A __________ ________ is a series of links connecting the many places of production and distribution and resulting in a final product that is then bought and sold on the market.
3. Timbuktu was a ______________ location, where goods traded on one mode of transport, camel, were transported to another mode of transport, boat.

HOW IS DEVELOPMENT DEFINED AND MEASURED?

4. Our modern notion of development is related to the ____________ ____________ and the idea that technology can improve the lot of humans. Through advances in __________, people can produce more food, create new products, and accrue material wealth.
5. Gross ___________ __________(GNP) is a measure of the total value of the officially recorded goods and services produced by the citizens and corporations of a country in a given year. It includes goods and services made both __________ and _________ the country's territory, and it is therefore broader than gross ____________ product (GDP), which encompasses only goods and services produced __________ a country during a given year.
6. In recent years, economists have increasingly turned to gross __________ _________ (GNI), which calculates the monetary worth of what is produced within a country plus income received from investments outside the country minus income payments to other countries around the world.
7. GNI is a limited measure because it includes only transactions in the ________ __________, the legal economy that governments tax and monitor. Quite a few countries have per capita

GNI of less than $1000 per year—a figure so low it seems __________ that people could survive.

8. A key component of survival in these countries is the __________ economy, the uncounted or illegal economy that governments do not _____ and keep track of, including everything from a garden plot in a yard to the black market to the illegal drug trade.
9. A high correlation between ________ and ________ _________ (Figure 10.4) means that instead of mobile phones equalizing Internet access for rich and poor countries, the technology can either reinforce or exacerbate the ________ _________ between rich and poor.
10. The ______________ _______ measures the proportion of dependents in the population relative to every 100 people of working age.
11. The overall dependency ratio of young and old relative to the working-age population can be _________ into an older person dependency ratio, population over the age of _____ relative to the working-age population, and a younger person dependency ratio, population ages birth to ____ relative to the working-age population.
12. At the summit, world leaders recognized the principal barriers to ___________ ____________ and identified eight key development goals to be achieved by the year 2015. They were:
    1. Eradicate extreme ______________ and hunger.
    2. Achieve universal ___________ education.
    3. Promote gender equality and _____________ women.
    4. Reduce child ____________.
    5. Improve _____________ health.
    6. Combat HIV/AIDS, _________, and other diseases.
    7. Ensure environmental ________________.
    8. Develop a global partnership for ________________.
13. The classic development model, one that is subject to each of these criticisms, is economist Walt Rostow's _____________ model.
14. Rostow's model assumes that all countries follow a similar path to development or modernization, advancing through ______ stages of development. In the first stage, the society is _____________, and the dominant activity is subsistence farming.
15. The second stage brings the ______________ of takeoff. New leadership moves the country toward greater flexibility, openness, and ___________. These changes, in turn, will lead to the third stage, __________. Urbanization __________, industrialization proceeds, and technological and mass-production breakthroughs occur.
16. Next, the economy enters the fourth stage, the ________ ___ __________. Technologies diffuse, industrial specialization occurs, and international ________ expands. Modernization is evident in key areas of the country, and population growth __________.
17. Finally, some countries reach the final stage in Rostow's model, high _______ ___________, which is marked by high _________ and widespread production of many goods and services.

HOW DOES GEOGRAPHICAL CONTEXT AFFECT DEVELOPMENT?

18. The continuation of colonial relationships after formal colonialism ends is called ______________, whereby major world powers continue to _______ the economies of the poorer countries, even though the poorer countries are now politically independent states.
19. Structuralists have developed a major body of development theory called ___________ theory, which holds that the political and economic relationships between countries and regions of the world control and limit the economic development possibilities of poorer areas.
20. *The Economist* reported that in 2011, ___countries have currencies (including China, Saudi Arabia, and Bangladesh) tied to the U.S. dollar: More than 40 countries peg the value of their currency to the U.S dollar, and __ countries have abandoned their currency and have completely adopted the U.S. dollar. The process of adopting the U.S. dollar as a country's currency is called __________.
21. Immanuel ______________ world-systems theory is attractive to geographers because it incorporates space (geography) and time (history) as well as ________ ___________ (politics) that shape the context in which development takes place.
22. Wallerstein's division of the world into a __________ structure—the core, periphery, and semiperiphery—helps explain the interconnections among places in the global economy.

WHAT ARE THE BARRIERS TO AND THE COST OF DEVELOPMENT?

23. Across the global periphery, as much as ________ of the population is 15 years old or younger (see Figure 10.5b), making the supply of adult, taxpaying laborers _____ relative to the number of dependents.
24. Lack of education for _______ is founded on and compounded by the assumption held not just in the periphery but in most of the world that girls will __________ their homes (and communities) when they marry and contribute to their husband's family and not their own. The views that girls are _____ important than boys and that girls cost a family money and provide little financial support are at the root of _________ ________________.
25. Mike Dottridge, a modern antislavery activist, explains that trafficking happens when "adults and children fleeing poverty or seeking better prospects are ______________, deceived, and bullied into working in conditions that they would ____ choose."
26. ____________ ____________ loans were part of a larger trend toward neoliberalism in the late twentieth century. _________________ derives from the neo-classical economic idea that government intervention into markets is inefficient and undesirable, and should be resisted wherever possible.
27. Political __________ and instability can greatly impede economic development. In peripheral countries, a wide divide often exists between the very wealthy and the poorest of the poor.
28. The ____________ case shows that in low-income countries, corrupt leaders can stay in power for decades because the people are ______ to rise up against the leader's extreme power or because those who have risen up have been killed or harmed by the leader's followers.

29. In their efforts to ________ new industries, the governments of many countries in the global periphery and semiperiphery have set up special manufacturing export zones called export processing zones (EPZs) which offer favorable tax, regulatory, and trade arrangements to foreign firms.
30. By 2006, ____ countries had established 3500 _____, and many of these had become major manufacturing centers. Two of the best known of these zones are the Mexican ___________ and the special economic zones of China.
31. In 1992, the United States, Mexico, and Canada established the North American ______ ________ Agreement (NAFTA), which prompted further industrialization of the border region.
32. Although the expansion and contraction of deserts can occur naturally and cyclically, the process of __________________ is more often exacerbated by humans destroying vegetation and eroding soils through the _______ of lands for livestock grazing or crop production.
33. All ___________ strategies have pros and cons, as is well illustrated by the case of tourism. _________ frequently strains the fabric of local communities as well. The invasion of poor communities by wealthier visitors can foster antipathy and ___________. Tourism can also have the effect of altering, and even debasing, _______ culture (see Chapter 4), which is adapted to suit the visitors' taste.

HOW DO POLITICAL AND ECONOMIC INSTITUTIONS INFLUENCE UNEVEN DEVELOPMENT WITHIN STATES?

34. Poverty is not ________ to the periphery. Core countries have _________ and peoples that are markedly poorer than others. On the Pine Ridge Indian Reservation in the northern _________ _________ of the United States, unemployment hovers at 80 percent, and more than 60 percent of the people live in poverty with a per capita income of just over $6000.
35. In both periphery and core, governments often invest in growing the economy of the __________ ________ so that it can act as a showcase for the country.
36. In many countries of the global economic periphery and semiperiphery, the capital cities are by far the ___________ and most economically _______________ cities in the state.
37. When a government or corporation builds up and concentrates economic development in a certain city or small region, geographers call that place an _________ ___ ______________.
38. ___________________ __________ (NGOs) are not run by state or local governments. Thousands of NGOs operate in the world today, from churches to charities such as _______ _________________. Each NGO has its own set of _______, depending on the primary concerns outlined by its founders and financiers.
39. The idea behind a ______________ program is simple: Give loans to poor people, particularly __________, to encourage development of small businesses.

Step 4: "Map It" Quiz: Use the maps from the text to answer the questions.

1. What two countries have the largest informal economies as a proportion of their GDP?
   A. China and India
   B. Nigeria and Sudan
   C. Panama and Bolivia
   D. Thailand and Vietnam
   E. Iraq and Iran

2. Which of the following regions has a value of 0–15 percent value of the informal economy compared to the GDP throughout the region?
   A. Europe
   B. Russia
   C. East Asia
   D. North America
   E. South America

3. Which region has the highest number of people 65 years of age and older compared to the population of 15- to 64-year-olds?
   A. North America
   B. Europe
   C. Subsaharan Africa
   D. Southeast Asia
   E. East Asia

4. Which region has the highest number of people 14 years and younger compared to the popiulation of 15- to 64-year-olds?
   A. North America
   B. Europe
   C. Subsarahan Africa
   D. Southeast Asia
   E. MIddle America

5. Which of the following regions had the most countries at a very low development level according to the Human Development Index?
   A. South America
   B. Southeast Asia
   C. South Asia
   D. Subsaharan Africa
   E. Russia

Step 5: AP-Style Practice Quiz

1. Which of the following is NOT true regarding peripheral countries and tourism?
   A. "Host" countries tend not to own or control the tourism infrastructure.
   B. Funds for hotel construction are often diverted from local needs.
   C. The tourist industry contributes substantially to the "host" country's development.
   D. Local leaders may have a stake in hotel/resort revenues.
   E. Tourists consume large quantities of scarce commodities such as food and water.

2. Mexico has established export processing zones with special tax, trade, and regulatory arrangements for foreign firms. These zones are referred to as:
   A. maquiladoras
   B. haciendas
   C. border cities
   D. NAFTA zones
   E. free trade areas

3. Which is NOT among the five stages of Rostow's development model?
   A. traditional
   B. takeoff
   C. high mass consumption
   D. collapse-decline
   E. drive to maturity

4. Even if the gross national income (GNI) per capita index is used to measure the well-being of a country, it will fail to show:
   A. growth in secondary industries (manufacturing)
   B. the distribution of wealth
   C. growth within tertiary industries (services)
   D. growth within primary industries (mining, forestry, agriculture, fishing)
   E. change in the economy over time

5. The principal structuralist alternative to Rostow's model of economic development is known as:
   A. the takeoff model
   B. the liberal model
   C. the modernization model
   D. the dependency theory
   E. grass-roots activism

6. Which of the following is NOT one of the Millennium Development Goals?
   A. Eradicate HIV/AIDS by the year 2025.
   B. Achieve universal primary education.
   C. Ensure environmental sustainability.
   D. Promote gender equality and empower women.
   E. Improve maternal health.

7. Which of the following is NOT associated with core production processes?
   A. technology
   B. low-wage labor
   C. education
   D. research and development
   E. modern cities

8. Which of the following does NOT make up a portion of Colombia's GNI?
   A. professional sports franchises
   B. tourism
   C. coffee production
   D. drug trafficking
   E. flower exports

9. A large component of survival in countries with low per capita GNI is:
   A. foreign aid
   B. the sales of resources
   C. the informal economy
   D. tourism
   E. prostitution

10. Which of the following is NOT true of microcredit programs?
    A. Repayment rates are high, hovering at 98 percent
    B. Many NGOs offer microcredit programs.
    C. Microcredit loans are given to poor people, particularly women.
    D. The programs tend to reinforce male dominance in society.
    E. The programs can also help alleviate malnourishment.

CHAPTER 11:
AGRICULTURE AND THE RURAL LANDSCAPE

Name: ______________________________ **Period** __________ **Date** ____________

Chapter Title: ____

Chapter # ______________________________ **Pgs.** ____________ **to** ____________

The Five Steps to Chapter Success

Step 1: Read the Chapter Summary below and preview the Key Questions.

Step 2: Complete the Pre-Reading Activity (PRA) for this chapter.

Step 3: Read the chapter and complete the guided worksheet.

Step 4: Read the maps and take the "Map It!"quiz

Step 5: Take an AP-style Practice Quiz

STEP 1: Chapter Summary and Key Questions

Chapter Summary

Agricultural production has changed drastically since the First Agricultural Revolution. Today, agricultural products, even perishable ones, are shipped around the world. Agriculture has industrialized, and in many places, food production is dominated by large-scale agribusiness. A major commonality between ancient agriculture and modern agriculture remains: the need to change. Trial and error were the norms of early plant and animal domestication; those same processes are at play in the biotechnology-driven agriculture of the contemporary era. Whatever the time period or process involved, agriculture leaves a distinct imprint on the cultural landscape, from land surveys to land ownership to land use. Globalization has made an imprint on landscapes and agribusiness. What is produced where is not simply a product of the environment and locally available plants; the modern geography of agriculture depends on factors ranging from climate and government regulations to technology and shifting global consumption patterns.

Key Questions

Field Note: Changing Greens	p. 311–313
1. What is agriculture, and where did agriculture begin?	p. 313–319
2. How did agriculture change with industrialization?	p. 320–325
3. What imprint does agriculture make on the cultural landscape?	p. 326–330
4. How is agriculture currently organized geographically, and how has agribusiness influenced the contemporary geography of agriculture?	p. 330–345

Step 2: Pre-Reading Activity (PRA)

1. Write down each of the Key Questions with the fewest pages and the most pages.

Key Question	# of Pages
What imprint does agriculture make on cultural landscape?	4
→ Question 4	15

2. After looking over the Key Questions and the Chapter Summary, write a few sentences about what you expect to learn in general in this chapter.

I expect to learn about the different agricultural revolutions that have occured in history.

3. How many world maps are there in this chapter? 5 (Go to Student Companion Website and print out organizers for help.)

4. Read the Field Note introduction of the chapter and list three specific facts you learned.

- Soybeans grow in western South Dakota
- Farmers w/ organic farming certification have great advantage
- USDA certification of organic products

5. Go to Step 1 and look at the Geographic Concepts. Create a list of terms you think you know and terms you need to know.

I THINK I KNOW	I NEED TO LEARN
seed crops	root crops
plant domestication	subsistence agricultural
GMO's	shifting cultivation
climatic regions	slash-and-burn agriculture

Step 3: Chapter 11 Guided Worksheet

Directions: As you read the chapter, fill in the blanks on the guided worksheet.

FIELD NOTE—CHANGING GREENS

1. Ready soybeans a particular genetically modified soybean that can grow in more arid regions of the country.
2. Counter to the genetically modified Roundup Ready crops, organic agriculture—the production of crops without the use of synthetic or industrially produced pesticides and fertilizers—is also on the rise in North America. In wealthier parts of the world, the demand for organic products has risen exponentially in recent years.
3. Although organic crops are grown everywhere, most organic foods are sold in the global economic core: in the United States, Canada, Japan, Europe, and Australia.

WHAT IS AGRICULTURE, AND WHERE DID AGRICULTURE BEGIN?

4. Agriculture is the deliberate tending of crops and livestock to produce food, feed, fiber, and fuel.
5. Economic activities that involve the extraction of economically valuable products from the earth, including agriculture, ranching, hunting and gathering, fishing, forestry, mining, and quarrying, are called primary economic activities.
6. Activities that take a primary product and change it into something else such as toys, ships, processed foods, chemicals, and buildings are secondary economic activities. Manufacturing is the principal secondary economic activity. Tertiary economic activities are those service industries that connect producers to consumers and facilitate commerce and trade or help people meet their needs.
7. Some analysts separate specialized services into quaternary and quinary economic activities, distinguishing between those services concerned with information or the exchange of money or goods (quaternary) and those tied to research or higher education (quinary).

8. In the United States, total agricultural production is at an all-time high, but the proportion of the labor force in agriculture is at an all-time low. Mechanization and efficiencies created by new technologies have led to a significant decrease in the number of workers needed in agricultural production.
9. Before the advent of agriculture, hunting, gathering. and fishing were the most common means of subsistence throughout the world.
10. Using tools and fire, human communities altered their environments, which helped to establish more reliable food supplies.
11. Saver, who spent a lifetime studying cultural origins and diffusion, suggested that Southeast and South Asia may have been the scene, more than 14,000 years ago, of the first domestication of tropical plants. There, he believed, the combination of human settlements, forest margins, and fresh water streams may have given rise to the earliest planned cultivation of root crops—crops that are reproduced by cultivating either the roots or cuttings from the plants (such as tubers, including manioc or cassava, yams, and sweet potatoes in the tropics).
12. The planned cultivation of seed crops, plants that are reproduced by cultivating seeds, is a more complex process, involving seed selection, sowing, watering, and well-timed harvesting. The cultivation of seed crops marked the beginning of what has been called the First Agricultural Revolution.
13. Some scholars believe that animal domestication began earlier than plant cultivation, but others argue that animal domestication began as recently as 8000 years ago—well after crop agriculture.
14. Subsistence agriculture—growing only enough food to survive—was the norm throughout most of human history.
15. Some subsistence farmers are sedentary, living in one place throughout the year, but many others move from place to place in search of better land. The latter engage in a form of agriculture known as shifting cultivation. This type of agriculture is found primarily in tropical and subtropical zones, where traditional farmers had to abandon plots of land after the soil became infertile.
16. One specific kind of shifting cultivation is slash-and-burn agriculture (also called swidden, milpa, or patch agriculture), reflecting the central role of the controlled use of fire in places where this technique is used.

HOW DID AGRICULTURE CHANGE WITH INDUSTRIALIZATION

17. For the Industrial Revolution to take root, a Second Agricultural Revolution had to take place—one that would move agriculture beyond subsistence to generate the kinds of surpluses needed to feed thousands of people working in factories instead of in agricultural fields.
18. New technologies improved production as well. The seed drill enabled farmers to avoid wasting seeds and to plant in rows, making it simpler to distinguish weeds from crops.
19. Studying the spatial patterns of land use around towns such as Rostock, von Thünen noted that as one moved away from the town, one commodity or crop gave way to another.

20. Nearest the town, farmers generally produced commodities that were perishable and commanded high prices, such as dairy products and strawberries.
21. In von Thünen's time, the town was still surrounded by a belt of forest that provided wood for fuel and building; but immediately beyond the forest the ringlike pattern of agriculture continued. In the next ring, crops were less perishable and bulkier, including wheat and other grains. Still farther out, livestock raising began to replace field crops.
22. The Third Agricultural Revolution is associated with the use of biotechnology to expand agricultural production.
23. The Third Agricultural Revolution relies on hybridization of seeds to produce a more stable crop in a variety of circumstances (wind resistant, drought resistant), intensified use of technology and irrigation, and expanded use of land either by not leaving it fallow or by farming on marginal land.
24. In the 1960s, the focal point of the Third Agricultural Revolution shifted to India, when scientists at a research institution in the Philippines crossed a dwarf Chinese variety of rice with an Indonesian variety and produced IR8.
25. This new rice plant had a number of desirable properties: It developed a bigger head of grain, and it had a stronger stem that did not collapse under the added weight of the bigger head. IR8 produced much better yields than either of its parents—giving rise to the Green Revolution.
26. The term *Green Revolution* refers to the use of biotechnology to create disease-resistant, fast-growing hybrid seeds—particularly of staple crops such as rice and wheat. The impact of the Green Revolution in India and other developing countries was so great that the term is often used as a synonym for the Third Agricultural Revolution.
27. A major debate has developed around GMOs. Proponents argue that GMOs can help feed an expanding world population and that hard evidence of negative consequences to their use is lacking. Opponents contend that GMO companies are releasing organisms into the environment without adequate understanding of their environmental health, or socioeconomic consequences.
28. They are not subsistence farmers in the strict sense, but the term *subsistence* is surely applicable to societies where farmers with small plots sometimes sell a few pounds of grain on the market but where poverty, indebtedness, and tenancy are ways of life.

WHAT IMPRINT DOES AGRICULTURE MAKE ON THE CULTURAL LANDSCAPE?

29. The pattern of land ownership seen in the landscape reflects the cadastral system—the method of land survey through which land ownership and property lines are defined.
30. The prevailing survey system throughout much of the United States, the one that appears as checkerboards across agricultural fields, is the rectangular survey system. The U.S. government adopted the rectangular survey system after the American Revolution as part of a cadastral system known as the township-and-range system.
31. Among the most significant are the metes-and-bounds survey approach adopted along the eastern seaboard, in which natural features were used to demarcate

irregular parcels of land. One of the most distinctive regional approaches to land division can be found in the Canadian Maritimes and in parts of Quebec, Louisiana, and Texas, where a long-lot survey system was implemented.

32. This system divided land into narrow parcels stretching back from rivers, roads, or canals. It reflects a particular approach to surveying that was common in French America.
33. In systems where one child inherits all of the land—such as those associated with the traditional Germanic practice of primogeniture, in which all land passes to the eldest son—parcels tend to be larger and farmers work a single plot of land.
34. Nucleated settlement is by far the most prevalent rural residential pattern in agricultural areas around the world.
35. Commercial farming has come to dominate in the world's economic core, as well as some of the places in the semiperiphery and periphery. Commercial farming is the agriculture of large-scale grain producers and cattle ranches, mechanized equipment, and factory-type labor forces.
36. One major impact of colonial agriculture was the establishment of monoculture (dependence on a single agricultural commodity) throughout much of the colonial world.
37. We owe this remarkable map to Wladimir Köppen (1846–1940), who devised a scheme called the Köppen climate classification system for classifying the world's climates on the basis of temperature and precipitation.
38. When comparing the world map of agriculture with the distribution of climate types across the world, we can see the correlation between climate and agriculture.
39. Colonialism profoundly shaped nonsubsistence farming in many poorer countries. Colonial powers implemented agriculture systems to benefit their needs, a practice that has tended to lock poorer countries into production of one or two "cash" crops.
40. When cash crops are grown on large estates, we use the term plantation agriculture to describe the production system.
41. As Figure 11.18 shows, by far the largest areas of commercial agriculture (1 through 4 in the legend) lie outside the tropics. Dairying (1) is widespread at the northern margins of the midlatitudes—particularly in the northeastern United States and in northwestern Europe.
42. Only one form of agriculture mentioned in the legend of Figure 11.18 refers to a particular climatic zone: Mediterranean agriculture (6).
43. Because of the high demand for drugs—particularly in the global economic core—farmers in the periphery often find it more profitable to cultivate poppy, coca, or marijuana plants than to grow standard food crops.
44. Consider the case of coffee, one the most important luxury crops in the modern world. Coffee was first domesticated in the region of present-day Ethiopia, but today it is grown primarily in Middle and South America, where approximately 70 percent of the world's annual production is harvested.
45. The push for fair trade production shows how social movements can influence agriculture. And fair trade goes beyond coffee. Dozens of commodities and products, ranging from tea, bananas, fresh cut-flowers, and chocolate to soccer balls, can be certified fair trade.

46. Agribusiness is an encompassing term for the businesses that provide a vast array of goods and services to support the agricultural industry. Agribusiness serves to connect local farms to a spatially extensive web of production and exchange.
47. Because of agribusiness, the range and variety of products on the shelves of urban supermarkets in the United States is a world apart from the constant quest for sufficient, nutritionally balanced food that exists in some places.
48. Commercial agriculture produces significant environmental changes. The growing demand for protein-rich foods and more efficient technologies are leading to overfishing in many regions of the world. In many places fish stocks are declining at an alarming rate.
49. In recent decades, the popularity of fast-food chains that serve hamburgers has led to the deforestation of wooded areas in order to open up additional pastures for beef cattle, notably in Central and South America.
50. Looking ahead, there is growing concern in the United States and beyond over the loss of fertile, productive farmlands to housing and retail developments.
51. As a result of the growing distance between farmers and consumers, geographers have sought to draw attention to food desserts—areas where people have limited access to fresh, nutritious foods.

Step 4: "Map It" Quiz: Use the maps from the text to answer the questions.

1. According to Figure 11.4, which of the following regions was NOT an area of agricultural innovation?
   A. North America
   B. Middle America
   C. Southwest Asia
   D. Southeast Asia
   E. South America

2. According to Figure 11.9, in which of the following areas does subsistence agriculture primarily exist?
   A. Europe
   B. North Africa and Southwest Asia
   C. South Asia
   D. Subsaharan Africa
   E. Australia

3. According to Figure 11.17, which of the following regions has the largest arid zone within it?
   A. North America
   B. North Africa and Southwest Asia
   C. South Asia
   D. Southeast Asia
   E. Subsaharan Africa

4. According to Figure 11.17, Indonesia is dominated by which of the following climates?
   A. Dry climate—Arid
   B. Humid Equatorial Climate—Dry winter
   C. Humid Equatorial Climate—No dry season
   D. Humid Temperate Climate—No dry season
   E. Humid Cold Climate—No dry season

5. According to Figure 11.18, which of the following regions has a dominant area of shifting cultivation?
   A. North America
   B. Middle America
   C. South America
   D. South Asia
   E. Australia

6. According to Figure 11.18, which of the following regions has a dominant area dedicated to nomadic and seminomadic herding?
   A. North Africa and Southwest Asia
   B. Subsaharan Africa
   C. South Asia
   D. Southeast Asia
   E. Australia

7. According to Figure 11.21, in which of the following areas of the United States does broiler chicken production occur the most?
   A. the Midwest
   B. the Southwest
   C. the Pacific Northwest
   D. the Northeast
   E. the South

Step 5: AP-Style Practice Quiz

1. In recent years, many wooded areas in ________ have been deforested to provide beef for hamburgers for fast-food chains in the United States.
   A. East and South Asia
   B. West Africa
   C. East Africa
   D. Central and South America
   E. Canada

2. Coffee was domesticated in Ethiopia. Today, 70 percent of production is in:
   A. Southeast Asia
   B. South Asia
   C. East Africa
   D. Middle and South America
   E. North America

3. The largest purchaser of fair trade coffee in the world is:
   A. Dunkin Donuts
   B. Starbucks
   C. Tim Horton's
   D. McDonald's
   E. Target

4. The rectangular land division scheme in the United States adopted after the American Revolution is quite unique. Its correct name is:
   A. the long-lot system
   B. the metes and bounds system
   C. the mile-grid system
   D. Franklin's system
   E. the township-and-range system

5. According to Spencer and Thomas, each agricultural hearth was associated with a local grouping of plants. For example, yams, sweet potatoes, and cassava are associated with the _______hearth.
   A. Meso-American
   B. Southeast Asian
   C. Southwest Asian
   D. Ethiopia-East African
   E. Amazonian

6. A form of tropical subsistence agriculture in which fields are rotated after short periods of crop production is:
   A. subsistence rice cultivation
   B. subsistence wheat cultivation
   C. shifting cultivation
   D. nomadic herding
   E. transhumance

7. Which two crops are most associated with the Green Revolution?
   A. yams and cassava
   B. bananas and oranges
   C. rice and wheat
   D. cotton and tobacco
   E. grapes and olives

8. Which is NOT an example of a primary economic activity?
   A. corn flake production
   B. iron ore production
   C. lobster fishing
   D. forestry
   E. petroleum extraction

9. In areas of shifting cultivation, the population:
   A. increases significantly
   B. cannot have a high density
   C. must be large enough to provide surplus labor
   D. never lives in permanent settlements
   E. practices an unsustainable form of agriculture

10. Colonial powers would make subsistence farmers:
    A. grow cash crops only
    B. farm on plantations in addition to farming their own land
    C. grow cash crops in addition to food crops the farmer needed to survive
    D. buy commercial fertilizer at fixed prices
    E. leave the land to work in factories

CHAPTER 12:
INDUSTRY AND SERVICES

Name: ______________________________ **Period** __________ **Date** ____________

Chapter Title: ____

Chapter # ____________________________ **Pgs.** ____________ **to** ____________

The Five Steps to Chapter Success

Step 1: Read the Chapter Summary below and preview the Key Questions.

Step 2: Complete the Pre-Reading Activity (PRA) for this chapter.

Step 3: Read the chapter and complete the guided worksheet.

Step 4: Read the maps and take the "Map It!"quiz

Step 5: Take an AP-style Practice Quiz

STEP 1: Chapter Summary and Key Questions

Chapter Summary

The Industrial Revolution transformed the world economically, politically, and socially. Many of the places where industrialization first took hold have since become deindustrialized, both with the relocation of manufacturing plants and with the outsourcing of steps of the production process domestically and offshore. With changing economics, places change. Some now look like ghost towns, serving merely as a reminder that industrialization took place there. Others have booming economies and are thriving, having kept industry or having successfully developed a service economy. Still other places are redefining themselves. In the next chapter, we consider another lasting effect of industrialization and deindustrialization: environmental change.

Key Questions

Field Note: Containing the World-Economy	p. 346–347
1. Where did the Industrial Revolution begin, and how did it diffuse?	p. 347–354
2. How have the character and geography of industrial production changed?	p. 355–371
3. How have deindustrialization and the rise of service industries altered global economic activity?	p. 371–377

Step 2: Pre-Reading Activity (PRA)

1. Write down each of the Key Questions with the fewest pages and the most pages.

Key Question	# of Pages
How have the character + geo of industrial...	16
How have deindustrialization and the rise of the service industry...?	6

2. After looking over the Key Questions and the Chapter Summary, write a few sentences about what you expect to learn in general in this chapter.

I expect to learn about the historical origins of the Industrial Revolution and the different features that have affected industrial processes today.

3. How many world maps are there in this chapter? 6 (Go to Student Companion Website and print out organizers for help.)

4. Read the Field Note introduction of the chapter and list three specific facts you learned.

- ports have less employees due to use of the crane
- larger ship = less money to transport containers
- San Francisco port not suitable for loading and unloading of containers

5. Go to Step 1 and look at the Geographic Concepts. Create a list of terms you think you know and terms you need to know.

I THINK I KNOW	I NEED TO LEARN
Rust Belt	technopole
deindustrialization	break-of-bulk point
commodity chain	intermodal connections
outsourcing	global sourcing

Step 3: Chapter 12 Guided Worksheet

Directions: As you read the chapter, fill in the blanks on the guided worksheet.

FIELD NOTE—CONTAINING THE WORLD ECONOMY

1. The container ship is the backbone of globalization and has dramatically changed the economic geography of the planet since the first one sailed in 1956. Before containers, a ship would arrive at port with various, odd-sized crates and boxes.
2. Hundreds of longshoremen would flock to the dock to unload the goods by hand. With containerization, ports now have relatively few employees who operate the high-tech cranes, moving standard-sized containers from ship to dock or dock to ship with precision.

WHERE DID THE INDUSTRIAL REVOLUTION BEGIN, AND HOW DID IT DIFFUSE?

3. The manufacturing of goods began long before the Industrial Revolution. In cottage industries, families in a community worked together, each creating a component of a finished good or the good itself.
4. The transition from cottage industries to the Industrial Revolution happened in the context of changing economies of scale.
5. Through the mass production of goods, brought about by the Industrial Revolution, Europe eventually flooded global markets with inexpensive products, burying cottage industries at home and in Asia.
6. Textile factories in the British Midlands, south of Manchester, took advantage of rivers and hills to power cotton spinning machines by water running downhill.
7. James Watt is credited with improving the steam engine by creating a separate chamber to house the steam and by perfecting the pistons and getting them to perform correctly.
8. During the early part of the Industrial Revolution, before the railroad connected nodes of industry and reduced the transportation costs of coal, manufacturing needed to be located close to coal fields. Manufacturing plants also needed to be connected to ports, where raw materials could arrive and finished products could depart.
9. With the advent of the railroad and steamship, Great Britain enjoyed even greater advantages over the rest of the world than it did at the beginning of the Industrial Revolution.
10. In the early 1800s, as the innovations of Britain's Industrial Revolution diffused into mainland Europe, the same set of locational criteria for industrial zones applied: sites needed to be close to resources and connected to ports by water.
11. The Rühr is connected to the port of Rotterdam, the Netherlands by the Rhine River. Each port has a hinterland, or an area from which goods can be produced, delivered to the port, and then exported.

12. By choosing a site, or location, in London, a manufacturing company put itself at the center of Britain's global network of influence. Paris was already continental Europe's greatest city, but like London, it did not have coal or iron deposits in its immediate vicinity.
13. When a railroad system was added to the existing network of road and waterway connections to Paris, however, the city became the largest local market for manufactured products for hundreds of miles.
14. London and Paris became, and remain, important industrial complexes not because of their coal fields but because of their commercial and political connectivity to the rest of the world.
15. Industrialization began to diffuse from Europe to the Americas and Asia in the nineteenth century, and secondary hearths of industrialization were established in eastern North America, western Russia and Ukraine, and East Asia.
16. Manufacturing in North America began in New England during the colonial period, but the northeastern States were not especially rich in mineral resources.
17. Industries developed along the Great Lakes where canal, river, and lakes connected with railroads on land to move resources and goods in and out of industrial centers.
18. The St. Petersburg region is one of Russia's oldest manufacturing centers.
19. Japan's dominant region of industrialization and urbanization is the Kanto Plain, which contains about one-third of the nation's population and includes the Tokyo–Yokohama–Kawasaki metropolitan area.

HOW HAVE THE CHARACTER AND GEOGRAPHY OF INDUSTRIAL PRODUCTION CHANGED?

20. Improvements in transportation and communication technologies are at the root of globalization. The improvement of sailing ships and navigation methods helped establish global trade routes and the first wave of colonialism.
21. Ford's idea that the dominant mode of mass production that endured from 1945 to 1970 is known as Fordist.
22. The Fordist period is marked by a surge in both mass production and mass consumption. On the Ford assembly line, machines replaced people, and unskilled workers instead of craftsmen worked on the assembly lines.
23. Under Fordist production, distance was a major consideration in the location of industry.
24. The presence of infrastructure, nearness to customers, and humid climate (which kept wood from cracking) were also reasons furniture manufacturers located in close proximity to one another in North Carolina.
25. Whenever furniture manufactures have considered locating outside of North Carolina and the Piedmont region or moving operations abroad, one of the key issues has been the friction of distance: the increase in time and cost that usually comes with increased distance over which commodities must travel.
26. Distance decay assumes the impact of a function or an activity will decline as one moves away from its point of origin.

27. Marshall explained why industries would cluster, and German economic geographer Alfred Weber (1868–1958) developed a basic model explaining where industries would cluster.
28. Weber's least-cost theory focused on a factory owner's desire to minimize three categories of costs. The first and most important of these categories was transportation. Weber suggested that the site where transportation costs are lowest is the place where it is least expensive to bring raw materials to the point of production and to distribute finished products to consumers.
29. The second cost was that of labor. Higher labor costs tend to reduce the margin of profit, so a factory farther away from raw materials and markets might do better if cheap labor compensates for the added transport costs.
30. Weber described the advantages that came about when similar industries clustered together, which he termed agglomeration.
31. As a result, in the latter third of the twentieth century many enterprises began moving toward a post-Fordist, flexible production model. The post-Fordist model refers to a set of production processes in which the components of goods are made in different places around the globe and then brought together as needed to assemble the final product in response to customer demand.
32. Through the process of commodification, goods that were not previously bought, sold, and traded gain a monetary value and are bought, sold, and traded on the market.
33. Tracing the production of televisions throughout the world over time helps us see how the global division of labor (also called the new international division of labor) currently works.
34. Time–space compression is based on the idea that developments in communication and transportation technologies have accelerated the speed with which things happen and have made the distance between places less significant.
35. With just-in-time delivery, this has changed. Rather than keeping a large inventory of components or products, companies keep just what they need for short-term production and new parts are shipped quickly when needed.
36. In the triangle of factors, the most important for lightweight consumer goods is a ready supply of low-cost labor. Being close to the raw materials is less of a concern, as shipping low-weight components is relatively inexpensive.
37. Each node, or connection point in a network, of the Nike network is functionally specialized, dependent on other nodes, and influenced by the niche it occupies in the network.
38. Outsourcing is now an umbrella term for globalized production in which a defined segment of the commodity chain is contracted abroad, either through business process outsourcing (BPO) or through global sourcing.
39. As the iPod example illustrates, multinational corporations frequently subcontract many of the steps in the production and retailing process to outside companies or subsidiaries, through BPO and global sourcing contracts, including the extraction of raw materials, engineering, manufacturing, marketing, distribution, and customer support.

40. Weber's location theory no longer works for most products, except those that rely on heavy raw materials.

41. Since World War II, major developments in transportation have focused on improving intermodal connections, places where two or more modes of transportation meet (including air, road, rail, barge, and ship), in order to ease the flow of goods and reduce the costs of transportation.

42. The WTO promotes freer trade by negotiating agreements among member states, typically dismissing import quota systems and discouraging protection by a country of its domestically produced goods.

43. Today major industrial complexes are not confined to areas near oil fields. Instead, a huge system of pipelines and tankers delivers oil and natural gas to manufacturing regions throughout the world.

44. The United States leads world demand and consumption not just in oil, but in natural gas as well.

45. As a result of advances in flexible production, over the last 30 years many older manufacturing regions have experienced deindustrialization, a process by which companies move industrial jobs to other regions, leaving the newly deindustrialized region to work through a period of high unemployment and, if possible, switch to a service economy.

46. Benefiting from the shift of labor-intensive industries to areas with lower labor costs, government efforts to protect developing industry, and government investment in education and training, the tigers emerged as newly industrialized countries (NICs).

47. Hong Kong's situational advantages contributed enormously to its economic fortunes. The colony became Mainland China's gateway to the world, a bustling port, financial center, and break-of-bulk point, where goods are transferred from one mode of transport to another.

48. Under state planning rules, the Northeast district (formerly known as Manchuria and now called Dongbei) became China's industrial heartland, a complex of heavy industries based on the region's coal and iron deposits located in the basin of the Liao River.

49. At the same time, the Northeast has become China's "Rust Belt." Many of its state-run factories have been sold or closed, or are operating below capacity. Unemployment is high, and economic growth has stalled.

HOW HAVE DEINDUSTRIALIZATION AND THE RISE OF SERVICE INDUSTRIES ALTERED THE ECONOMIC GEOGRAPHY OF PRODUCTION?

50. The expanding service sector in the core economies is only one aspect of the changing global economy.

51. Deindustrialization and the growth of the service economy unfolded in the context of a world-economy that was already characterized by wide socioeconomic disparities. Only areas that had industry could deindustrialize, of course, and at the global scale the wealthier industrial regions were the most successful in establishing a postindustrial service economy.

52. This region of the United States, which used to be called the Manufacturing Belt, is now commonly called the Rust Belt, evoking the image of long-abandoned, rusted-out steel factories.

53. The Sun Belt is the southern region of the United States, stretching through the Southeast to the Southwest. Both the population and economy of this region have grown over the last few decades, as service sector businesses have chosen to locate in areas such as Atlanta and Dallas where the climate is warm and the local laws welcome their presence.

54. Many of the call centers for technical help for computers and related industries (software, hardware) are located in India and the Phillipines.

55. A high-technology corridor is an area designated by local or state government to benefit from lower taxes and high-technology infrastructure, with the goal of providing high-technology jobs to the local population.

56. The area became what geographers call a growth pole, not just because other high-technology businesses came to Silicon Valley, but because the concentration of these businesses spurred economic development in the surrounding area.

57. The resulting collection of high-technology industries produced what Manuel Castells, Peter Hall, and John Hutriyk call a technopole, an area planned for high technology where agglomeration built on a synergy among technological companies occurs.

58. Service economies have their own vulnerabilities. Tourism can fall off in the face of economic downturns or natural hazards, and office work can be outsourced to distant places.

Step 4: "Map It" Quiz. Use the maps from the text to answer the questions.

1. According to Figure 12.2, Britain's access to sources of capital flow in 1775 were from these two regions:
   A. Subsaharan Africa and South Asia
   B. North America and South America
   C. Southeast Asia and South America
   D. North America and South Asia
   E. Australia and Russia

2. According to Figure 12.8, which of the following regions did NOT have major industrial activity?
   A. North America
   B. Europe
   C. Russia
   D. East Asia
   E. South Asia

3. According to Figure 12.13, which of the following regions does NOT include a Nike apparel, equipment or footware factory?
   A. North America
   B. East Asia
   C. Russia
   D. Southeast Asia
   E. Subsaharan Africa

4. According to Figure 12.17, the commodity chain for an iPod Processor includes all of the following regions EXCEPT:
   A. East Asia
   B. Europe
   C. North America
   D. South Asia
   E. South America

5. According to Figure 12.18, these three countries produce the most oil in the world on a daily basis:
   A. Saudi Arabia, United Arab Emirates, and Iran
   B. Russia, China, and Iraq
   C. Iraq, Saudi Arabia, and Brazil
   D. The United States, Saudi Arabia, and Russia
   E. Libya, Angola, and Saudi Arabia

Step 5: AP-Style Practice Quiz

1. Over 50 percent of the goods entering Europe come through two ports in:
   A. Luxembourg
   B. Belgium
   C. Netherlands
   D. Germany
   E. France

2. Service industries are commonly referred to as _____ industries.
   A. primary
   B. secondary
   C. tertiary
   D. quaternary
   E. quinary

3. Russia's "Detroit," located southeast of Moscow, is:
   A. Kiev
   B. St. Petersburg
   C. Volgograd
   D. Rostov
   E. Nizhni Novgorod

4. Japan's dominant industrial region is:
   A. Kitakyushu
   B. Toyama
   C. Kanto Plain
   D. Kansai
   E. Shikoku

5. Fast, flexible production of small lots of products with outsourcing around the world is referred to as:
   A. Fordist
   B. post-Fordist
   C. socialist
   D. colonial production
   E. just-in-time

6. The increase in time and cost with distance is referred to as:
   A. production costs
   B. distribution costs
   C. friction of distance
   D. distance decay
   E. frustration

7. When Alfred Weber published his book Theory of the Location of Industries (1909), what did he select as the critical determinant of regional industrial location?
   A. availability of labor
   B. nearby markets
   C. costs of labor
   D. transportation costs
   E. political influence

8. The type of manufacturing that is more likely to be located in peripheral countries is:
   A. technical design
   B. labor-intensive
   C. low-labor needs
   D. high-tech
   E. low value-added

9. The most important locational factor for the service sector is:
   A. energy
   B. transportation
   C. market
   D. labor
   E. climate

10. Technopoles, a collection of high-technology industries, can be found in a number of countries. Which of the following is NOT a region containing one of these countries?
    A. eastern Asia
    B. India
    C. Australia
    D. North America
    E. Africa

CHAPTER 13:
THE HUMANIZED ENVIRONMENT

Name: ______________________________ **Period** __________ **Date** ____________

Chapter Title: ____

Chapter # ____________________________ **Pgs.** ____________ **to** ____________

The Five Steps to Chapter Success

Step 1: Read the Chapter Summary below and preview the Key Questions.
Step 2: Complete the Pre-Reading Activity (PRA) for this chapter.
Step 3: Read the chapter and complete the guided worksheet.
Step 4: Read the maps and take the "Map It!"quiz
Step 5: Take an AP-style Practice Quiz

STEP 1: Chapter Summary and Key Questions

Chapter Summary

What will the future be like? Many would agree with geographer Robert Kates, who foresees a "warmer, more crowded, more connected but more diverse world." As we consider this prospect, we must acknowledge that global environmental changes illustrate the limits of what we know about our planet. Global environmental change is not always anticipated and is often nonlinear. Some changes are "chaotic" in the sense that future conditions cannot be reliably predicted. Nonlinearity means that small actions in certain situations may result in large impacts and may be more important than larger actions in causing change. Thresholds also exist in many systems, which, once past, are irreversible. Irreversible changes occur, for example, when the habitat for a species is diminished to the point where the species quickly dies off. Unfortunately, we may not be able to identify these thresholds until we pass them. This leaves open the possibility of "surprises"—unanticipated responses by physical systems.

The complexity and urgency of the environmental challenge will tax the energies of the scientific and policy communities for some time to come. Geography must be an essential part of any serious effort to grapple with these challenges. The major changes that are taking place have different origins and spatial expressions, and each results from a unique combination of physical and social processes. We cannot simply focus on system dynamics and generalized causal relationships. We must also consider emerging patterns of environmental change and the impacts of differences from place to place on the operation of general processes. Geography is not the backdrop to the changes taking place; it is at the very heart of the changes themselves.

Key Questions

Field Note: Disaster along Indian Ocean Shores	p. 434–436
1. How has Earth's environment changed over time?	p. 437–443
2. How have humans altered Earth's environment?	p. 443–452
3. What are the major factors contributing to environmental change today?	p. 452–459
4. What policies are being adopted in response to environmental change?	p. 459–462

Step 2: Pre-Reading Activity (PRA)

1. Write down each of the Key Questions with the fewest pages and the most pages.

Key Question	# of Pages

2. After looking over the Key Questions and the Chapter Summary, write a few sentences about what you expect to learn in general in this chapter.

3. How many world maps are there in this chapter? _____ (Go to Student Companion Website and print out organizers for help.)

4. Read the Field Note introduction of the chapter and list three specific facts you learned.

____

____

____

____

____

____

____

5. Go to Step 1 and look at the Geographic Concepts. Create a list of terms you think you know and terms you need to know.

I THINK I KNOW	I NEED TO LEARN

Step 3: Chapter 13 Guided Worksheet

Directions: As you read the chapter, fill in the blanks on the guided worksheet.

FIELD NOTE—DISASTER ALONG OCEAN SHORES

1. Many headlines referred to the __________ as a tidal wave, but a tsunami has nothing to do with the tides that affect all oceans and seas. A tsunami results from an __________ __________ involving a large displacement of the Earth's crust.
2. Tsunamis of the magnitude of 2004 are not common, but as the deadly tsunami that struck the northeast coast of __________ in 2011 reminds us, the hazard is continuous.
3. The tsunami that struck coasts along the _________ ________ from Indonesia to Somalia and from Thailand to the Maldives resulted from a violent ______________ measuring more than 9.0 on the (10-point) Richter scale off the west coast of the island of Sumatra (Indonesia).
4. For example, the release of ____________________ (CFCs) in the Northern Hemisphere in past decades contributed to a hole in Earth's ozone layer over Antarctica.

HOW HAS EARTH'S ENVIRONMENT CHANGED OVER TIME?

5. Human ______________ of the environment continues in many forms today. For the first time in history, however, the combined impact of humanity's _____________ and _____________ actions is capable of producing environmental changes at the global scale.
6. The twentieth-century ________ in the size of the human population, combined with a rapid escalation in ____________, magnifies humanity's impact on Earth in unprecedented ways.
7. One of them, the climatologist–geographer _________ ___________, used his spatial view of the world to make a key contribution. His __________________ _________ hypothesis required the preexistence of a supercontinent, which he called __________, which broke apart into the fragments we now know as Africa, the Americas, Eurasia, and Australia.
8. Around 1500 million years ago, green algae started to spread across Earth's ocean surfaces, and as their colonies grew, their _______________ (the conversion of carbon dioxide and

water into carbohydrates and oxygen through the absorption of sunlight) raised the atmosphere's __________ content.

9. Physical geographers hypothesize that the earliest phase of Pangaea's fragmentation was also the most __________, that the plate separations that started it all were driven by built-up, extreme heat below the supercontinent, but that the motion of the plates has since slowed down. The ___________ _______ of Fire—an ocean-girdling zone of crustal instability, volcanism, and earthquakes—is but a trace of the paroxysm that marked the onset of Pangaea's breakup.
10. The _______________ epoch, which began 2 million years ago (Figure 13.6), was marked by long glaciations and short, warm interglacials.
11. After this warm-up came the most recent glaciation of the Pleistocene, the __________________ _____________, which left its mark on much of the Northern Hemisphere.
12. A volcano, ________ ________, erupted on the Indonesian island of Sumatra. This was not just an eruption: The entire mountain exploded, sending millions of tons of debris into orbit, obscuring the sun, creating long-term darkness, and altering ______________ ________.
13. The Wisconsinan Glaciation eventually gave way to a full-scale interglacial, the current warm interlude that has been given its own designation, the ____________. Global warming began about 18,000 years ago, and for the next 6000 years, temperatures _________ ____________.
14. _______________ struck all over Europe, just at a time when more people were clustered in towns than ever before. The ___________ record, pieced together from farmers' diaries (wine- growers' diaries are especially useful), _______ ________ research (dendochronology), ice cores, contemporary writings, illustrative paintings, and surviving sketches and drawings, justifies the designation of the post–1300 period as a shift in the direction of reglaciation.
15. In North America, our growing understanding of the _________ _______ _______ helps explain why the _______________ colony collapsed so fast, a failure attributed by historians solely to ineptitude and lack of preparation.
16. Given the enormous quantities of ____________ poured into the planet's atmosphere as the Industrial Revolution gathered momentum, how large is the human contribution to the associated _______________ ________ (that results when greenhouse gases trap heat and raise temperatures)?

HOW HAVE HUMANS ALTERED EARTH'S ENVIRONMENT?

17. Biologists estimate that as many as a million types of organisms inhabit Earth, perhaps even more. Most have _______ yet been identified, classified, or studied. No species, not even the powerful dinosaurs, ever affected their environment as much as ___________ do today.
18. Some _______________ __________ is more obvious because it takes place around human habitats, such as cutting forests and emitting pollutants into the atmosphere. Less obvious environmental stress takes place away from dense concentrations of humans, including ________________ __________, burying toxic wastes that contaminate groundwater

supplies, and dumping vast amounts of ____________ into waterways and the world's oceans.

19. Resources that are replenished even as they are being used are _____________ resources, and resources that are present in __________ quantities are _________________ resources. Water, essential to life, is a ________________ resource.
20. Much of that water is lost through runoff and evaporation, but enough of it seeps downward into porous, water-holding rocks called ______________ to provide millions of _________ with steady flows.
21. One of the great _______________ disasters of the twentieth century occurred in Kazakhstan and Uzbekistan, whose common boundary runs through the __________ Sea. Streams that fed this large body of water were diverted to irrigate the surrounding desert, mainly for ______________ __________ production.
22. Textbooks teach that __________ is a constant whose distribution is sustained through the ______________ cycle, where water from oceans, lakes, soil, rivers, and vegetation evaporates, condenses, and then precipitates on landmasses.
23. Much of that water is lost through ___________ and ________________, but enough of it seeps downward into porous, water-holding rocks called _____________ to provide millions of wells with steady flows. In the United States alone, it is estimated that there is ____ ________ as much water stored in aquifers as there is precipitation falling on the land surface every year.
24. Textbooks teach that water is a constant whose distribution is sustained through the ________________ ________, where water from ___________, lakes, soil, rivers, and vegetation evaporates, condenses, and then ________________ on landmasses.
25. Earth's atmosphere is a ______ ______ of air lying directly above the lands and oceans. We depend on the atmosphere for our ____________: We breathe its oxygen; it shields us from the destructive rays of the sun; it moderates temperatures; and it carries _____________ from the oceans over the land, sustaining crops and forests and ______________ soils and wells.
26. While estimates of the degree of human-induced __________ ________ differ, climate records from recent decades show that global temperatures are ____________, which is why climate change is sometimes called global warming.
27. A by-product of the enormous volume of pollutants spewed into the atmosphere is ______ ______. Acid rain forms when _______ __________ and ________ __________ are released into the atmosphere by the burning of fossil fuels (coal, oil, and natural gas).
28. The world's _________, especially those of lower and middle latitudes, play a critical role in the __________ cycle. Atmospheric oxygen is consumed by _________ processes as well as by _________ activities. Forests counteract this loss through ______________ and related processes, which release oxygen into the atmosphere. The destruction of vast tracts of forest is called _______________.
29. _______ _____________ is caused by a variety of factors: __________ are allowed to graze in areas where they destroy the natural vegetation; lands ______ _______ to sustain farming are plowed, and wind erosion follows.
30. The United States is one of the largest producers of ________ _______, debris, and garbage discarded by those living in cities, industries, mines, and farms.

31. It is useful to draw a distinction between _______ ________, which are dangerous because of chemicals, infectious materials, and the like, and _____________ _______, which are of two types: low-level radioactive wastes, which give off small amounts of radiation and are produced by industry, ___________, research facilities, and nuclear power plants; and high-level radioactive wastes, which emit strong radiation and are produced by _________ ________ plants and nuclear weapons factories.
32. A significant change that is related to all of the developments discussed so far is the accelerating loss of _______________.
33. Species are becoming ________ at a rapid rate. It is difficult to say exactly ______ ______________extinctions are occurring, since we do not know how many species there are. What is clear, however, is that although extinction is a natural process, humans have dramatically ______________ rates of extinction, particularly over the last few hundred years.

WHAT ARE THE MAJOR FACTORS CONTRIBUTING TO ENVIRONMENTAL CHANGE TODAY?

34. Environmental change occurs at all levels of _________, from local to global. For example, deforestation has ________ effects by ________________ the diversity of species even in a small area.
35. ____________ _____________ are interested in how environmental issues such as _______________ are affected by the ways in which political, economic, social, and ecological circumstances play out in individual places.
36. To underscore the ___________ _______________ in environmental impact on humans, we can consider two maps of ___________ ____________ hot spots published by the Earth Institute at Columbia University and the World Bank in a 2005 report.
37. Thus, when a devastating _______________ hit the Kobe region in Japan in 1995, there was enormous property damage, but fewer than ___________ people died. By contrast, when an earthquake of a similar magnitude struck _________ in 2010, well over __________ people lost their lives.
38. The ______________ countries account for only a modest fraction of the human population, but they make far greater ___________ on Earth's resources than do their counterparts in poorer countries.
39. As global _____________ of consumer goods increases, the market for luxury goods has similarly expanded as more people around the world move into __________-class lifestyles.
40. We are continually developing ________________ that we hope will improve our standard of living, protect us against ____________, and allow us to work more efficiently. But these technologies come at a __________. Resource extraction practices such as _____________ and logging, which provide the materials to produce technologies, have created severe environmental _______________.
41. Each innovation in ________________ has required increased resource use, not only to make the vehicles that move people and goods, but also to build and maintain the related _________________—roads, railroad tracks, airports, parking structures, repair facilities, and the like.

42. Transportation is also implicated in global environmental change—albeit sometimes ______________. Advances in transportation have produced significant pollution, as seen in the extent of ______ ________ along major shipping lanes.
43. As populations grow, so does the demand for __________, and we can expect that over the coming decades energy production will __________ to meet the increased demand.
44. Rising energy prices have made it economical to use a costly technique called hydraulic ______________, or fracking, to reach these pockets. Fracking operations inject a high-pressure fluid (typically water mixed with sand and chemicals) into deep-rock formations to create small fissures and release ____________ _______.
45. Concerns over the long-term implications of a decline in ______ revenue in Kuwait have led to efforts to find an alternative source of wealth: potable __________. In a part of the world that can go for months without ________, water is a most precious resource.
46. Rare earth elements are in demand because they are used not only in _______ _________ but also in alternative energy cars, computers, screens, _____________ ____________ light bulbs, cell phones, MRI machines, and advanced weapons systems.

WHAT IS THE INTERNATIONAL RESPONSE TO CLIMATE CHANGE?

47. The extent and rapidity of recent environmental changes have led to the adoption of numerous ___________ aimed at protecting the environment or ____________ the negative impacts of pollution.
48. Environmental pollution ____________ political boundaries, and people sometimes move across those boundaries in response to environmental pressures.
49. The GEF funds projects related to six issues: loss of ____________, climate change, protection of international waters, depletion of the _________ layer, land degradation, and persistent organic pollutants.
50. The biodiversity convention is a step ___________ in that it both affirms the vital significance of preserving biological diversity and provides a framework for ___________ toward that end. However, the agreement has proved _____________ to implement.
51. However, a naturally occurring ozone layer exists in the ______________ (between 30 and 45 km altitude).
52. International cooperation began in 1985 with the negotiation of the Vienna Convention for the _______________ of the Ozone Layer.
53. Specific targets and timetables for the phaseout of production and consumption of _______ were defined and agreed upon as part of the international agreement known as the ___________ Protocol, which was signed in September 1987 by 105 countries and the European Community.
54. In 1997, the _________ Agreement set a target period of 2008–2012 for the _______ _________, the European Union, and Japan to cut their greenhouse gas emissions by 7, 8, and 6 percent, respectively, below 1990 levels. _________ the United States nor China, the world's two largest emitters of carbon dioxide, ___________ the Kyoto Protocol.
55. The United States continues to be the largest producer of _________ _________ emissions per person in the world.

56. One-fifth of the world's population lives in regions confronting water ___________. Yet to date there have been ______ conflicts among states over water.
57. Despite the many examples of cooperation, water management challenges ___________. In many cases monitoring is ____________, enforcement mechanisms are ___________, and provisions do not exist to address more extreme variations in water availability.

Step 4: "Map It" Quiz: Use the maps from the text to answer the questions.

1. According to Figure 13.5, most active volcanos are located in:
   A. Greenland
   B. the Atlantic Ocean
   C. the Arctic Ocean
   D. the Indian Ocean
   E. the Pacific Ocean

2. According to Figure 13.16, the risks of mortality due to a natural disaster resulting from drought are found in which region?
   A. Subsaharan Africa
   B. North America
   C. Middle America
   D. North Africa and Southwest Asia
   E. Australia

3. According to Figure 13.16, the risks of economic loss due to drought, hydro and geophysical, are highest in which region?
   A. North America
   B. Subsaharan Africa
   C. North Africa and Southwest Asia
   D. Australia
   E. Russia

4. According to Figure 13.23, carbon dixiode emissions were highest in:
   A. the United States
   B. China
   C. Russia
   D. Germany
   E. Australia

Step 5: AP-Style Practice Quiz

1. In the early 1980s the Food and Agriculture Organization of the United Nations undertook a study of the rate of depletion of tropical rain forests and determined that _______ percent had already been affected by cutting.
   A. 24
   B. 34
   C. 44
   D. 54
   E. 64

2. The United States is the most prolific producer of solid waste. Studies estimate that the United States produces about _____ pounds of solid waste per person per day.
   A. 1.5
   B. 4.5
   C. 5.5
   D. 7.3
   E. 8.1

3. The world's highest precipitation totals are in:
   A. equatorial and tropical areas
   B. midlatitude regions
   C. high latitudes
   D. subtropical regions
   E. elevations above 5,000 feet

4. The climatic record documenting the beginning of the Little Ice Age was partially pieced together by using farmer's diaries. Those of _______ were most useful.
   A. dairy farmers
   B. Catholic monks
   C. grain farmers
   D. vegetable growers
   E. wine growers

5. Climatologist-geographer Alfred Wegener used his spatial view of the world to develop the theory of:
   A. relativity
   B. the hydrologic cycle
   C. continental drift
   D. earth rotation
   E. plate subduction

6. The boundaries of crustal plates (theory of plate tectonics) are associated with:
   A. deserts
   B. earthquakes and volcanoes
   C. ice caps
   D. Plains regions
   E. mountain building

7. Plant life and photosynthesis began about 1.5 billion years ago and increased the ________ level in the atmosphere.
   A. CO_2
   B. nitrogen
   C. methane
   D. sulfur
   E. O_2

8. Fifty times as much as water is stored in ________ in the United States as falls as precipitation each year.
   A. reservoirs
   B. aquifers
   C. streams
   D. lakes
   E. glaciers

9. One of the great ecological disasters of the twentieth century occurred in Uzbekistan and Kazakhstan and involves the:
   A. Black Sea
   B. Lake Baikal
   C. Aral Sea
   D. Caspian Sea
   E. Lake Balqash

10. Forests affect the atmosphere through their role in:
    A. global warming
    B. the production of CO_2
    C. desertification
    D. the oxygen cycle
    E. decomposition

CHAPTER 14:
GLOBALIZATION AND THE GEOGRAPHY OF NETWORKS

Name: ______________________________ **Period** __________ **Date** ____________

Chapter Title: ____

Chapter # ______________________________ **Pgs.** ____________ **to** ____________

The Five Steps to Chapter Success

Step 1: Read the Chapter Summary below and preview the Key Questions.
Step 2: Complete the Pre-Reading Activity (PRA) for this chapter.
Step 3: Read the chapter and complete the guided worksheet.
Step 4: Read the maps and take the "Map It!"quiz
Step 5: Take an AP-style Practice Quiz

STEP 1: Chapter Summary and Key Questions

Chapter Summary

Globalization has been compared to a runaway train blowing through stations leaving much of the world to stare at its caboose. Yet this description is not entirely accurate. Globalization is a series of processes, not all of which are headed in the same direction. Even those processes headed down the globalization track are often stopped, sent back to the previous station, or derailed. The globalization track is not inevitable or irreversible (in the words of O'Loughlin, Staeheli, and Greenberg). Many of the most important globalization processes take place within networks of global cities (see Chapter 9), of places linked by popular culture (see Chapter 4), of governments (see Chapter 8), of trade (see Chapter 12), and of development (see Chapter 10). People and places are found all along these networks, and just as globalization influences people and places, those same people and places influence globalization's trajectory and future.

Key Questions

Field Note: Happiness Is in the Eye of the Beholder	p. 407–409
1. How have identities changed in a globalized world?	p. 409–411
2. What is globalization, and what role do networks play in globalization?	p. 412–415
3. How do networks operate in a globalized world?	p. 416–420

Step 2: Pre-Reading Activity (PRA)

1. Write down each of the Key Questions with the fewest pages and the most pages.

Key Question	# of Pages

2. After looking over the Key Questions and the Chapter Summary write a few sentences about what you expect to learn in general in this chapter.

3. How many world maps are there in this chapter? _____ (Go to Student Companion Website and print out organizers for help.)

4. Read the Field Note introduction of the chapter and list three specific facts you learned.

____

____

____

____

____

____

____

5. Go to Step 1 and look at the Geographic Concepts. Create a list of terms you think you know and terms you need to know.

I THINK I KNOW	I NEED TO LEARN

Step 3: Chapter 14 Guided Worksheet

Directions: As you read the chapter, fill in the blanks on the guided workshee

FIELD NOTE—HAPPINESS IS IN THE EYE OF THE BEHOLDER

1. As geographer Yi Fu Tuan said, "_________ make places." Each place is an imprint of _________, a reflection of diffusion, and a dynamic entity. Each place has its own ________ that makes it unique.
2. It is important not just to understand that the world is ___________, but to appreciate that the uniqueness of places cuts against the ________________that circulate about them.

HOW HAVE IDENTITIES CHANGED IN A GLOBALIZED WORLD?

3. In the 1990s, at the launch of the digital revolution, psychologists predicted that people would have __________ social skills because of the lack of personal or face-to-face interaction in the ____________ _______.
4. The idea that people who _____ ______ personally know each other and likely never will are linked and have shared experiences, including __________, tragedy, sorrow, and even joy, draws from Benedict Anderson's concept of the nation as an ____________ community.
5. Foote drew from extensive fieldwork that he conducted while visiting hundreds of landscapes of _________ and violence in the United States to show how people mark or do not mark tragedy, both immediately with spontaneous ____________ and in the longer term with permanent __________.
6. Foote realized that the ways sites are memorialized or not _______ over time and across a multitude of circumstances, depending on whether ___________ is available, what kind of structure is to be built, _______ is being remembered (only those who died or also those injured?), whether the site represents a socially contested event (which often happens when racism is involved), and whether people ________ to remember the site.

WHAT IS GLOBALIZATION, AND WHAT ROLE DO NETWORKS PLAY IN GLOBALIZATION?

7. Whether you are in favor of or opposed to globalization, we all must recognize that globalization is "neither an ___________ nor an _____________ set of processes," as John O'Loughlin, Lynn Staeheli, and Edward Greenberg put it.
8. The backbone of economic globalization is _________; so, debates over globalization typically focus on trade.
9. The view that free trade raises the wealth of all countries involved underpins a set of neoliberal policies known as the _________________ ____________.
10. Manuel Castells defines __________ as "a set of interconnected nodes" without a center.

11. Access (or lack of access) to information technology networks creates time–space compression, which means that ____________ ____________, such as global cities (especially in the core), are __________ interconnected than ever through communication and transportation networks, even as other places, such as those in the periphery, are farther ____________.

12. A major divide in access to information technology— sometimes called the __________ __________—is both a hallmark of the current world and an example of the ___________ outcomes of globalization.

HOW DO NETWORKS OPERATE IN A GLOBALIZED WORLD?

13. The term network defines any number of _________________ across the globe, whether transportation, educational, financial, or social.

14. Social networks, especially Facebook and Twitter, were credited with making ______________ in Tunisia and ___________ possible—first, through protest rap music and second, through construction and completion of plans for protest.

15. NGO _______________ ____________ serve as a counterbalance to the power of the major decision makers in the world, states, international financial institutions, and corporations.

16. Participatory development— the idea that ________ should be engaged in deciding what development means for them and how to achieve it—is another response to top-down decision making. Stuart Corbridge has studied how the global ________ for participatory development has encouraged the government of _______ to enact participatory development programs.

17. Today's ___________ encompass much more than print, radio, and television. With technological advances, media include entertainment, music, video games, ___________media sites, smart phone apps, and ___________ networks.

18. A _____________ _____________ corporation is one that has ownership in all or most of the points along the production and consumption of a commodity chain.

19. Vertical integration also helps media giants attract and maintain customers through __________, or the cross promotion of vertically integrated goods. For example, because of the vertical integration of _________, you can visit Walt Disney World's Animal Kingdom to catch the Festival of the Lion King, based on the Disney Theatrical Production that was based on the Walt Disney Picture, and while you are waiting in line, you can play the Disney ______ "Where's My Water" on your smartphone.

20. ___________ _____________ of media changes the geography of the flow of ideas around the globe by limiting the ultimate number of ______________, that is, people or corporations with control over access to information.

21. As a result of the extraordinary growth of __________, including Twitter, Weibo, and Qzone, on the Internet (1.3 billion microblog accounts in China and 271 million active accounts on Twitter), tight gatekeeping is much more ____________.

22. With ______________ integration, similar products are owned by one company, but they are branded separately so that consumers may think they are separate companies. Horizontal integration is common in __________ companies and housewares. Williams-Sonoma, West Elm, and Pottery Barn are separate stores in a mall, but they are all owned by the ________ ______________ company.
23. According to geographer Steven Schnell (2007), one of the reasons the number of farmers in the United States has increased is the growth in the number of _______________ supported agriculture groups, known as CSAs.
24. Through a _______, a farmer and consumers create a network whereby both assume ________. Consumers pay for a share of the farmer's __________, typically fruits and vegetables, __________ the growing season begins.

Step 4: "Map It" Quiz: Use the maps from the text to answer the questions.

1. According to Figure 14.2, the Gross National Happiness is highest in which of these regions?
   A. North America
   B. Europe
   C. Russia
   D. Subsarahan Africa
   E. Middle America

2. According to Figure 14.7, which of the following regions did not have a city that was connected to New York City?
   A. East Asia
   B. South America
   C. Southeast Asia
   D. Europe
   E. North America

Step 5: AP-Style Practice Quiz

1. According to Manuel Castells, a set of interconnected nodes is a(n):
   A. transport system
   B. circulation manifold
   C. network
   D. communication nexus
   E. synergy

2. The study of global cities showed that ______ is the most globally linked city in the world.
   A. New York
   B. Tokyo
   C. London
   D. Chicago
   E. Miami

3. More than anything else, globalization is driven by:
   A. cultural convergence of media
   B. resource scarcities
   C. population growth
   D. trade
   E. popular culture

4. The idea that locals should be engaged in deciding what development means for them and how to achieve it is known as:
   A. synergy
   B. structuralism
   C. international division of labor
   D. social networks
   E. participatory development

5. When one company, for example, a clothing company, buys several similar companies, you have an example of:
   A. horizontal integration
   B. vertical integration
   C. a commodity chain
   D. globalization
   E. diseconomies of scale

6. The phenomenon in which two or more discrete influences or agents acting together create many more benefits together than by acting alone is known as:
   A. synergy
   B. symbiosis
   C. integration
   D. gatekeeping
   E. networking

7. Media corporations that integrate ownership in a variety of points along the production and consumption chain are examples of:
   A. vertical integration
   B. television networks
   C. longitudinal cooperation
   D. monopolies
   E. diversification

8. Media's power as information gatekeepers has been undercut by:
   A. local television stations and newspapers
   B. social networks and blogs
   C. a decline in newspaper subscription
   D. growth in functional illiteracy
   E. self-censure because of FCC threats about indecency

9. The government of China works with foreign Internet companies to limit domestic access to foreign websites that the government finds threatening—a form of censure is which search engine companies like Google comply. In this role, the government of China is the ultimate:
   A. dictator
   B. guardian of morality
   C. agent of change
   D. representative of the will of people
   E. gatekeeper

10. Many antiglobalizationists are opposed to all of the following EXCEPT:
    A. increasing government-supported public services
    B. privatization of state-owned entities
    C. the opening of financial markets
    D. liberalization of trade
    E. the encouragement of direct foreign investment

Part 3: Preparing for the AP Human Geography exam

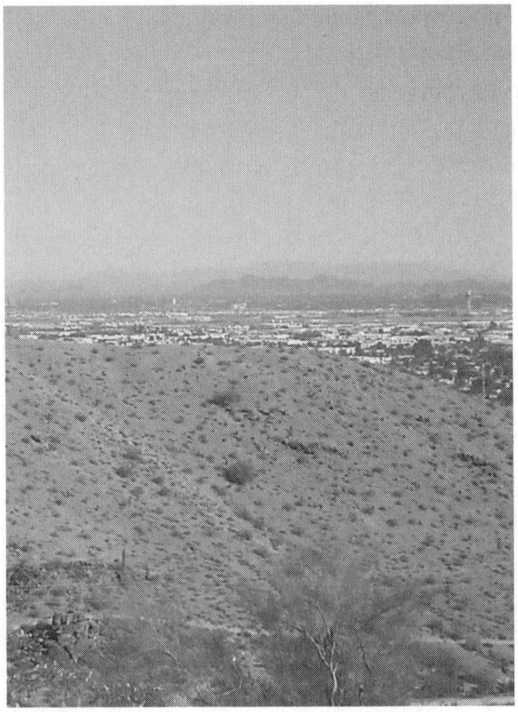

Purpose

The purpose of Part 3 of the workbook is to prepare for the AP Human Geography (APHG) exam. The APHG exam offers you an opportunity to demonstrate the knowledge and skills you have learned during your coursework and exam prep.

This section will give you some tools that are additional to the tips you found in your textbook.

We have divided this Part into four sections:

A. Anatomy of a Multiple-Choice Question
B. Anatomy of a Free-Response Question
C. Practice Exam #1
D. Practice Exam #2

Phoenix, Arizona. This is one of the fastest growing cities in the United States, and this picture illustrates the desert landscape. What environmental issues might there be concerning this trend?

SECTION 1: ANATOMY OF A MULTIPLE- CHOICE QUESTION (MCQ)

You may not have expected an anatomy lesson when you got this book. But an anatomy lesson is exactly what we are about to give. Let's break down what a multiple-choice question (MCQ) and a free response question look like. We will also dissect each question type to give you strategies for success on the APHG exam!

There are many ways APHG exam question writers may ask a MCQ. The following exercise is intended to give you some skills to attack MCQs.

First things first: If you have read an entire MCQ and are ***completely*** sure of the correct answer, then jump in and answer it. However, if you are even a little unsure about a question, use some of these techniques to help get you to the answer. As with anything in life, practice makes perfect. Go through the following exercises and then take the practice exams and use these skills such as key words, process of elimination, and length of answer as some examples of how you can get a leg up on answering a question.

SAMPLE A

PAY CLOSE ATTENTION TO SIMILAR SPELLINGS

Efforts by three or more countries who give up some measure of sovereignty to forge associations for common advantage and goals is known as:

a. superinternationalism
b. internationalism
c. supranationalism
d. intranationalism
e. neocolonialism

Don't ever miss a question because you chose an answer too quickly. Supranationalism is often mispronounced and misspelled. Many students in a hurry would choose answer A, when answer C is correct.

KEY - C

SAMPLE B

MANY TIMES ONE WORD IS ALL YOU NEED TO FOCUS ON

The map below, known for its distortion of the high latitudes, is a:

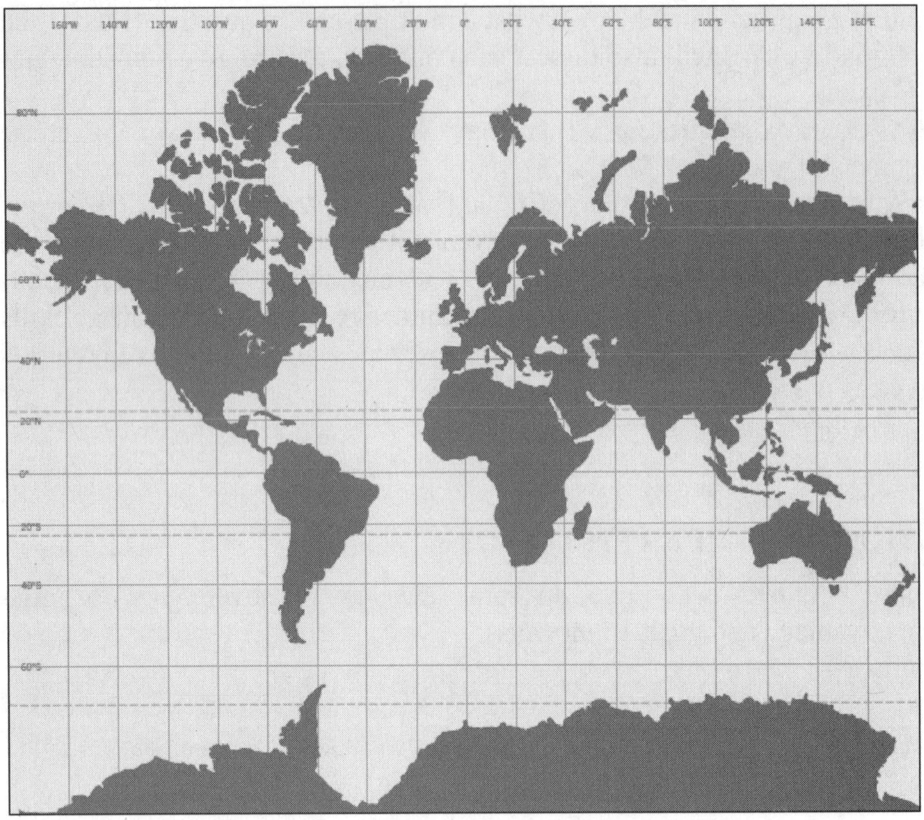

Source: © Fouberg, E. H., Murphy, A. B., and de Blij, H. J. *Human Geography, Tenth Edition.* (Hoboken, NJ: John Wiley & Sons,), p. A-5.

a. Robinson projection
b. Mercator projection
c. Isoplethic
d. Equal Area projection
e. Cartogram

In this question, the word "distortion" is the key to answering the question. Check out Antarctica on the map—it's almost as big as the rest of the world! Talk about distorted! Although all map projections have distortions to varying levels, the Mercator is known for its significant distortions in both of the high latitudes. The word "distortion" just about answers this question for you.

KEY - B

SAMPLE C

PROCESS OF ELIMINATION WITH SIMILAR COMPONENTS IN THE POSSIBLE ANSWERS

Which of the following correctly lists the usual hierarchy of political and/or urban entities in order from the largest to the smallest?

a. empire, county, province, nation-state
b. province, empire, nation-state, county
c. empire, nation-state, province, county
d. county, nation-state, province, empire
e. empire, nation-state, county, province

Too many times students know the material they are being asked about. The problem comes when all the possible answers are similar In a question like this, the key is to slow down. On the APHG exam, simply find the first answer that is patently wrong and cross it out. For example, it is well known that a *county* is smaller than an *empire*. Therefore, choice D could be ruled out immediately. Province is surely smaller than an empire. So eliminate choice B. Now you are down to three answers—A, C, and E. From this point, use common sense to get to the logical answer.

KEY - C

SAMPLE D

TO SKIP OR NOT TO SKIP

An entity where important global financial functions, international company headquarters, and a polarized social structure are located is indicative of:

a. forward capitals
b. edge cities
c. primate cities
d. world cities
e. entrepôts

Suppose you have no idea what an entrepôt or world city is. This will happen on the APHG exam. Have you ever heard the phrase, "Discretion is the better part of valor?" If you haven't, it means choosing to wait and act later is many more times more times more advantageous than acting immediately. If you have no clue about a question, it is usually better to just skip it and come back to it later. Many times you will encounter other terms and concepts on the test which will help you remember or understand a term you didn't understand in the first reading. Therefore, skip a question like this and come back to it when you have more time to think about it.

KEY - D

SAMPLE E

MORE PROCESS OF ELIMINATION and ANSWER LENGTH

Which of the following characteristics do Switzerland, Canada, and New Zealand currently share?

a. low population-growth rates
b. megalopolis urban systems
c. high infant-mortality rates
d. membership in the European Union (EU)
e. more than 10 percent of the population involved in sheep farming

It is important to remember that the APHG exam is written and constructed by professional exam writers and developers. One of the keys to a fair and well-written question is answer choices that are similar in appearance. That means all of the answers will generally be the same length. Sometimes, though, a question may have one answer that is longer than the other four choices. In a question like the one above, look at the longest answer. It could be the correct one simply because it provides the most information. Before conceding the longest answer as the correct one, it is always best to go through the process of elimination first.

KEY - E

SAMPLE F

NOPE, IT'S NOT AN OLD KEVIN BACON MOVIE—IT'S JUST COMMON SENSE

Footloose industries:

a. tend to be highly capital intensive in nature
b. are reliant upon all of Weber's location factors
c. can locate in most any place regardless of site or situation
d. have experienced sharp declines due to computers
e. are shoe factories that have relocated offshore

One of the things that is cool about human geography is that many of the terms truly describe themselves. Keep that in mind as you answer any question that has a geographic term as the focus. If you don't know what footloose industries are, just go with what seems to be common sense. Being *Footloose* like Kevin Bacon (old movie version) or Kenny Wormald (new movie version) just doesn't make sense in this question, but an industry being able to locate anywhere easily, or be footloose—well, that does make sense.

KEY - C

SAMPLE G

SUPPOSE THERE WAS A COMMANDMENT, "KNOW HOW THY MODELS WORK—NOT JUST WHAT THEY LOOK LIKE!"

Which of the following is useful for describing a settlement node whose primary function is to provide support for the population in its hinterland?

a. von Thünen's model of land use
b. concentric zone model
c. core-periphery model
d. Rostow's model of economic development
e. Christaller's model of central place

Although knowing what a model looks like is important, knowing what a model is about and does is more important. Rarely will you be asked to simply identify a model from its appearance. Most times you will be asked questions that *apply* to or *interpret* scenarios from the model. Look at Sample G—you are not asked about the model's appearance or construction. The question asks you how the model is ***used***.

KEY - B

SAMPLE H

STUDY THE OLD APHG EXAMS—THIS ONE IS A MULTIPLE-CHOICE VERSION OF FRQ #2 FROM THE 2001 APHG EXAM. THE POSSIBLE ANSWERS ARE ITEMS FROM THE FRQ RUBRIC.

Which of the following was NOT a reason for rapid suburbanization in the United States after World War II?

a. mass production of the automobile
b. reduction in long-distance commuting
c. expansion of home construction
d. expansion of the interstate highway system
e. availability of low down payment terms and long-term mortgages

You might study FRQs and FRQ rubrics from past APHG exams. Obviously, it is a good way to study for FRQs. But it also is a way to study for MCQs. Sample H is simply an FRQ that has been turned into an MCQ. Answers a, c, d, and e are correct items from the FRQ rubric. Note that answer choice b starts with a negative word, while the other answers are positive. This is a good test-taking technique to use throughout any MCQ exam.

KEY - B

SAMPLE I

BE ABLE TO CONNECT GEOGRAPHERS' NAMES TO THEIR WORK

Wilbur Zelinsky attempted to define cultural landscapes/regions by using information found in:

a. signs
b. ethnicities
c. cameras
d. journals
e. phonebooks

This question is very straightforward—provided you have studied your significant geographers and their work. Students may focus on knowing a geographic model or tool and forget to associate it with who created that model or tool.

KEY - E

SAMPLE J

SOME QUESTIONS ARE VERY DIFFICULT—YOU HAVE TO KNOW SEVERAL THINGS TO GET A QUESTION LIKE THIS RIGHT. BUT IT MIGHT NOT BE AS DIFFICULT AS YOU FIRST THINK.

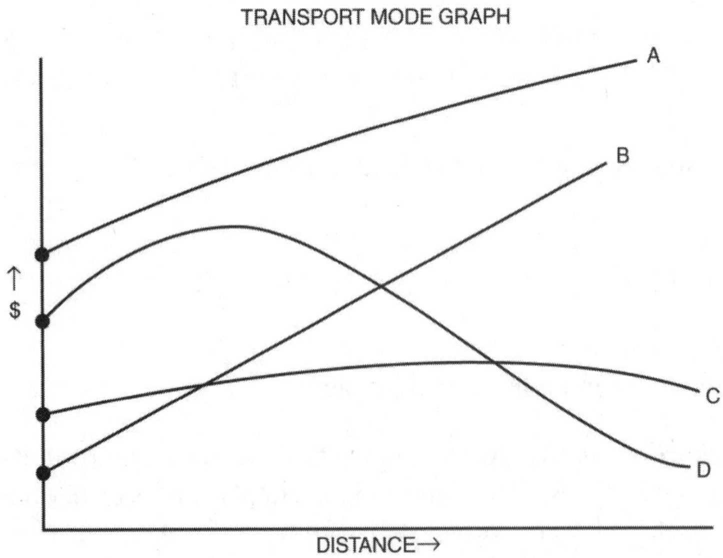

Source: © Paul T. Gray, Jr.

Use the graph above and your knowledge of transport modes and costs; which of the following is MOST correct?

a. The terminal costs are highest for mode B.
b. Mode A is the cheapest way to transport goods.
c. Air transport is the likely type for Mode C.
d. B is the best long-haul transport mode.
e. Mode D is very expensive for short-distance use.

First, this question has stimulus material. What that means is look at the graph, photo, map, diagram, or chart and see what this question might be about. Next, look at the question itself. In this question, you are asked to interpret what is happening in the diagram. Just to help you out on the diagram, A is air transport, B is truck transport, C is rail transport, and D is water or sea transport. Answering this question is all about the process of elimination. Go item by item to keep or throw out a potential answer. Again, you would need to know the specific characteristics, advantages, and disadvantages of each transport mode to correctly answer the question. Still, as challenging as this question appears to be, you could answer it using your x- and y-axis analysis skills. Look at answer E and back up at the chart. Wouldn't it be true that Mode D is an expensive (see the y-axis) choice for a short- (see the x-axis) haul shipment?

KEY - E

SECTION 2: ANATOMY OF A FREE RESPONSE QUESTION

Like MCQs there are many ways APHG exam question writers may ask a free response question (FRQ). The following exercise is intended to give you some skills to dissect and then attack FRQs.

Use what you have learned in this workbook and the AP version of the 11th edition Fouberg, Murphy and deBlij textbook about FRQs. There are lots of tips for identifying types of MCQs, key words, and other helpful strategies for writing success.

Be sure you listen to the exam proctor's instructions. With regard to one of the steps, the proctor will tell you to read the directions on how to answer an FRQ. Be sure to do so!

FRQs require a more deliberate approach than the MCQs because FRQs have more moving parts and variables. The first requirement for success on the FRQ section is to have a plan of attack for the 75 minutes you have to answer the three questions in this section. Let's look at some ways to use that time wisely by attacking the FRQs in a systematic way. In other words, you need a plan before you get to the FRQ section.

FRQ Battle Plan

You are told to open the exam, and now the 75 minute clock is running.

A. OUTLINING

1. Spend five minutes looking over the three questions.
2. Make some preliminary notes on each question. Write down terms and concepts; then draw out a model or anything that helps you organize your thoughts for that question.
3. IMPORTANT NOTE: Anything you write on the page where the question is printed is NOT scored. If you want any of your notes to be scored, be sure to move them over to the lined, answer sheet paper.
4. Before the five minutes is up, determine which question you think is the easiest and which is the most difficult for you to answer.

B. ANSWER THE QUESTION YOU BELIEVE IS THE EASIEST

1. Look at your watch or the clock on the wall in the testing room. Allow 10–15 minutes to answer the question you believe to be the easiest. This approach allows you to have success and gets you thinking geographically. This should help you as you go through the other two questions. This may be question 1, 2, or 3. Order does not matter—just answer the one you believe you know the most about first.
2. Underline, circle, or otherwise note key words. Look at the verbs—they tell you what to do, how much to write, and how deep to get. Look for the quantity you are being asked to do—one example, two examples, and so on.

3. Now begin answering the question. Use complete sentences (no, the exam is not graded for correct grammar and spelling) in your answers. This helps you answer using complete thoughts. It also keeps you from writing in bullets. Bullet form writing is not allowed on the APHG exam per the instructions you read. Bulleted answers are NOT scored!
4. In your answer, give only what is asked for. Too many times students put information into a question which they are simply not asked to do.
5. Remember to keep to your 10–15 minute time frame for your first question. At 15 minutes, move to the next question. If you finish before 15 minutes—good deal!

C. ANSWER THE QUESTION YOU BELIEVE IS THE NEXT EASIEST

1. You have 15 to 20 minutes to answer this question.
2. Again, this can be question 1, 2, or 3; order does not matter.
3. Repeat steps 2–4 from Section B above.
4. Be mindful of your 15- to 20-minute time frame for the second question. At 20 minutes, move to the next question. If you finish before 20 minutes, that's ok!

D. ANSWER THE QUESTION YOU BELIEVE IS THE HARDEST

1. You have 20–25 minutes to answer this question.
2. Order does not matter.
3. Repeat steps 2–4 from Section B above.
4. Remember not to over your 25 minute limit
5. If you use the maximum time allowed on the outline and each question, you will still have time left!

E. REVIEW WHAT YOU HAVE WRITTEN ON ALL THREE QUESTIONS

1. Even if you used your maximum time allotments on the outline and questions, you still have 5 minutes left
2. Use whatever time you have remaining to review your answers.
3. Scan the questions again to make sure you read the true intent of what has been asked of you.
4. Once you have looked it over again and are satisfied with your work, sit back and enjoy the success you have just had due to your hard work all year!

F. OTHER DOs and DON'Ts ON THE FRQs

1. **Question Asks for Examples**—If the question asks you to name three examples of something, understand that only the first three you give will be scored (this is part of the general exam instructions). For example, let's say the question asks for three examples of supranationalism; your answer is "NAFTA, MERCOSUR, Walmart, and African Union." You gave four answers, and the question asked for three. NAFTA, MERCOSUR, and African Union are supranational organizations; Walmart is not. Your paper would get credit for NAFTA and MERCOSUR, and no points would be awarded for Walmart. The answer of African Union would not be scored even though it is correct.

2. **Striking Out an Answer**—Let's say you write an example or sentence that you suddenly believe to be a wrong answer. You strike through that example, sentence, or even paragraph. If you strike through or in any way "line out" an answer or part thereof, it will not be scored. Even if the answer you had was correct and the reader can clearly see it, that portion will not be scored. Be careful.
3. **Time Frames**—No, the APHG exam is certainly not a history test. However, many questions will ask about geographic issues framed in a particular time. For example, the exam might ask about nation-states in the "late twentieth century" or about technology "developed in the past 40 years." Be sure your answer addresses only the geographic issues in that time frame.
4. **Know your A, B, Cs—Organize Your Answers by Section in ABC Format** - If you organize your answers in a coherent way, you are much more likely to write an answer that will achieve a higher score. Each question will have an A and B and perhaps a C, D, or even and E part. Be sure to put your answers for each section clearly labeled with that letter. Again, it keeps you organized, but it also allows the reader to find your answer easily and give you the credit you are seeking.

Some questions in the following exam are not covered in the Fouberg, Murphy, de Blij textbook. Similarly, there are items on the actual APHG Exam that you may not have studied. Therefore, it is important to study the APHG Course Outline as well as your textbook. If some of the following items or concepts are not familiar to you, review the text and workbook, or use an outside source to help you learn them.

SECTION 3: AP HUMAN GEOGRAPHY
EXAM ONE

You should allow 60 minutes to choose the BEST answer for each of the following items.

1. Which branch of geography focuses on natural landforms, climate, soils, and vegetation of the Earth?
   a. cultural geography
   b. human geography
   c. locational geography
   d. physical geography
   e. political geography

Use the quote from a National Council for Geographic Education newsletter, *Perspective,* to answer the following question.

> **The following is a quote from *Geography in the News* reported in September 2003: "The SARS (Severe Acute Respiratory Syndrome) virus is a highly contagious disease. New infections seem to radiate out from the epicenter. However, the virus may leapfrog to new centers, as infected individuals travel along transportation routes to other cities and towns. Rural residents with few contacts with major cities tend to avoid the virus until nearly the end of its diffusion cycle."**

2. According to the reading, SARS affects rural residents in what appears to be BEST described by which form of diffusion?
   a. stimulus
   b. hierarchical
   c. reverse hierarchical
   d. voluntary
   e. contagious

3. The map on the right, known for its distortion of the high latitudes, is a(n):

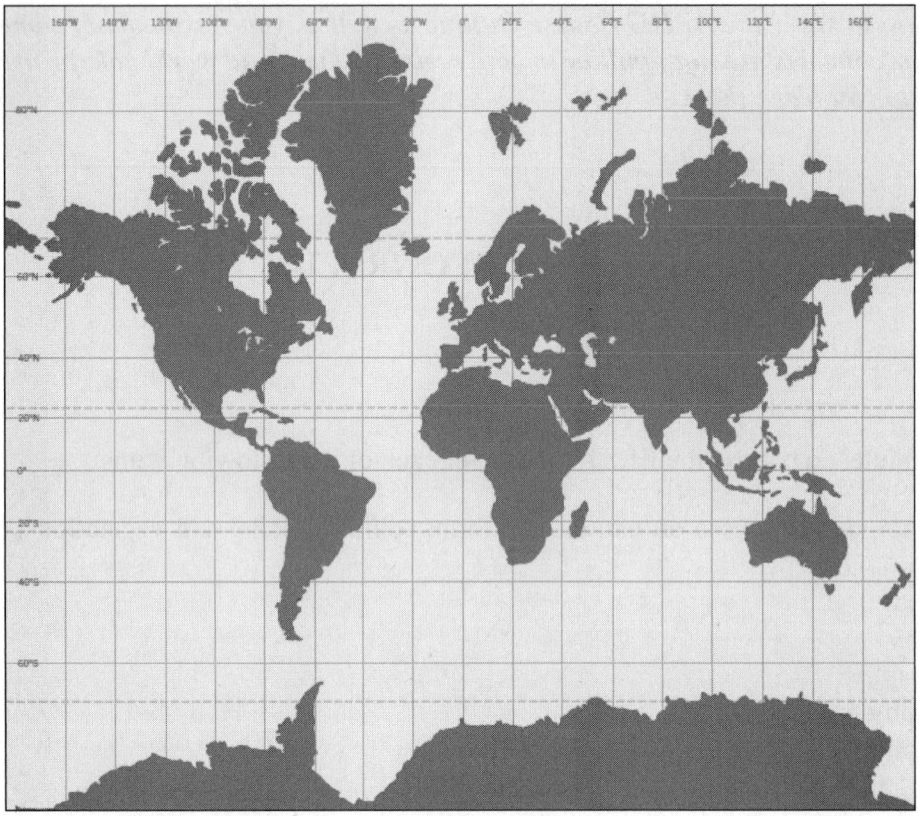

Source: © Fouberg, E. H., Murphy, A. B., and de Blij, H. J. *Human Geography, Tenth Edition.* (Hoboken, NJ: John Wiley & Sons,), p. A-5.

a. Robinson projection
b. Mercator projection
c. isopleth
d. equal area projection
e. cartogram

4. The location of a place in relationship to other places or features around it is called:
a. absolute location
b. site location
c. relative location
d. actual location
e. perceived location

5. The diagram on the right BEST indicates the concept of:

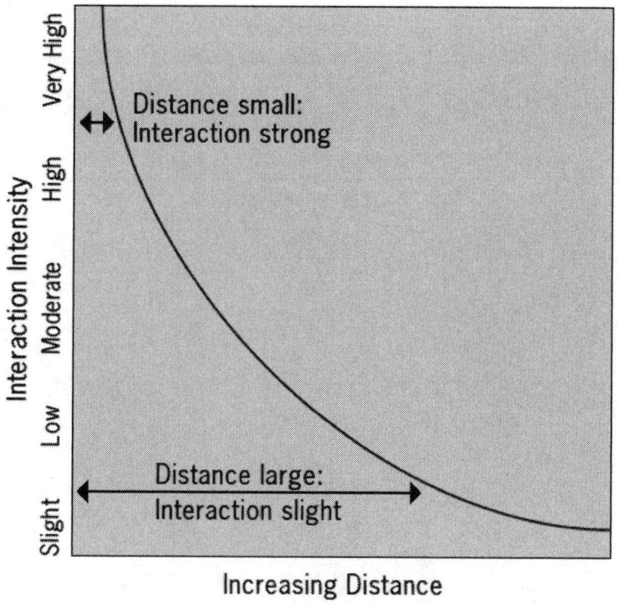

Source: © Fouberg, Murphy, and de Blij, H. J. *Human Geography*

a. hierarchical diffusion
b. assimilation
c. barriers to diffusion
d. distance decay
e. acculturation

6. Mental (or cognitive) maps are largely:
   a. accurate and reflect actual information on printed maps
   b. made up of cartographic and physiologic information
   c. an accurate analysis of accessible data
   d. based on the imagined experiences of an individual
   e. largely developed from first-hand experiences in a place

7. The layering of geographic data by computers into datasets is known as:
   a. GPS
   b. ENSO
   c. RSS
   d. GIS
   e. GNI

8. Which map projection is exhibited on the right?

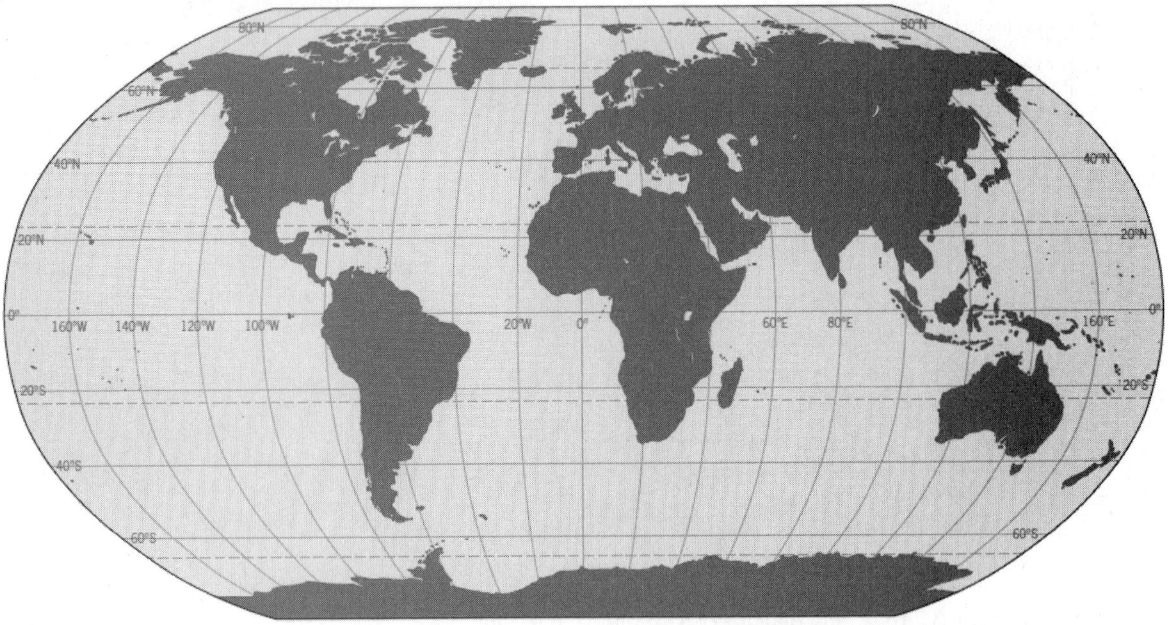

Source: © Fouberg, Murphy, and de Blij, *Human Geography, Tenth Edition,* p. A-6

a. Mercator
b. Goode's Interrupted
c. Robinson
d. Cartogram
e. Choropleth

9. Which of the following statements about migration is INCORRECT?
a. Many migrants leave their homes because of war.
b. Environmental problems cause many people to migrate.
c. Most migrants leave their homes because of high taxes.
d. Many migrants go to poor countries that cannot accommodate more people.
e. Most migrants in the world leave to pursue a "better life."

10. The approximate growth rate needed to sustain replacement of a population is:
    a. 5.8 percent
    b. 7.1 percentc. 10.5 percent
    d. 4.6 percent
    e. 2.1 percent

Use these diagrams to answer question 11.

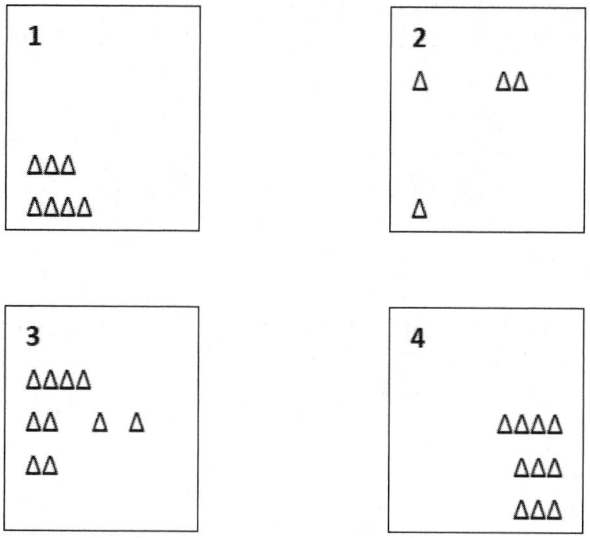

11. Using your knowledge of population density and distribution, which two of the four boxes have the highest *density* of triangles?
    a. 1, 3
    b. 3, 4
    c. 1, 2
    d. 4, 1
    e. 2, 3

12. The world's population can best be described as generally concentrated in:
    a. East Asia and Southern Europe
    b. Northwestern North America and South Asia
    c. South Asia and East Asia
    d. Europe and Eastern South America
    e. Western Africa and Southeast Asia

13. Contrary to Malthus's predictions in 1798, food production has since grown exponentially because of all of the following EXCEPT:
    a. the Green Revolution
    b. mechanization
    c. technology
    d. genetic engineering
    e. increased farmland

14. The statistic that reports the number of deaths per thousand people in a given year in a population is called the:
    a. total fecundity or fertility rate
    b. crude death or mortality rate
    c. adjusted population level
    d. actual growth rate
    e. age-sex mortality rate

15. Assuming the Demographic Transition Model has five stages, the actual ***transition*** is represented by
    a. stages three and four
    b. stages one and two
    c. stages two and three
    d. stages one and three
    e. stages one and five

16. Population growth is exceptionally fast from both migration and total fertility in which of the following cities?
    a. Lagos
    b. London
    c. New York City
    d. Tokyo
    e. Paris

17. One of historical geography's major examples of agriculturally induced migration involved the movement of hundreds of thousands of citizens to the United States from which European country in the 1830s and 1840s?
    a. Ireland
    b. England
    c. Belgium
    d. Spain
    e. Greece

18. One of the "laws" of migration as derived by Ravenstein states that:
    a. urban residents are more migratory than inhabitants of rural areas
    b. urban residents tend to be less religious than rural residents
    c. rural inhabitants hardly ever migrate
    d. urban residents are less migratory than inhabitants of rural areas
    e. rural people tend to farm more than urban people

19. A family decides to move to another region or place a long distance away, but finds a suitable place to settle before reaching their original intended destination. This is called:
    a. temporary settlement
    b. luck option
    c. intervening opportunity
    d. reverse distance decay
    e. sequent occupance

20. The number of deaths per 1000 population between the first and fifth birthdays is known as:
    a. natural increase rate
    b. infant mortality rate
    c. crude death rate
    d. total death rate
    e. child mortality rate

21. A country that has reached a stage where the population has very low growth, such as Germany or Japan, should have a population pyramid that is _________-shaped.
    a. bell
    b. apple
    c. rectangular
    d. pyramid
    e. circular

22. From the list below, choose the country with the largest number of languages spoken.
    a. China
    b. Brazil
    c. India
    d. Pakistan
    e. Canada

23. The two theories of the Proto-Indo European language dispersal through Europe are the conquest theory and the__________________ theory:
    a. agriculture
    b. migration
    c. trade routes
    d. missionary
    e. technology

24. As of 2003, the largest ethnic minority group in the United States is made up of:
    a. Asians
    b. Hispanics
    c. Turks
    d. Native Americans
    e. Americans of African ancestry

25. Any common language spoken by peoples of diverse speech is today called a(n):
    a. official language
    b. monolingual language
    c. pidgin language
    d. lingua franca
    e. idiomatic tongue

26. The island in the Mediterranean Sea that had to be partitioned because two cultures, the Greeks and Turks, could not get along is:
    a. Malta
    b. Sicily
    c. Corsica
    d. Sardinia
    e. Cyprus

27. The branch of Christianity that has been resurrected in Russia, eastern Europe, and many Slavic countries and is growing rapidly is:
    a. Catholicism
    b. Protestantism
    c. Eastern Orthodox
    d. Shaker
    e. Unitarianism

28. Islam dominates in:
    a. Southeast and East Asia
    b. South Asia and South Africa
    c. West and Central Africa
    d. Northern Africa and Southwest Asia
    e. Sub-Saharan Africa and South America

29. By the late 1990s, the fastest growing of the world religions had become:
    a. Christianity
    b. Islam
    c. Buddhism
    d. Hinduism
    e. Judaism

30. A simplified form of a lingua franca is known as a(n):
    a. pidgin
    b. euphemism
    c. Creole
    d. dialect
    e. idiom

31. Which of the following SUPPORTS the following position statement: *English will continue to be the global lingua franca in the year 2100.*
    a. Total Fertility Rates among English-speaking peoples are generally low.
    b. There are many linguistic revival movements going on around the world today.
    c. The computer/Internet allows non-English languages more opportunity for diffusion.
    d. English is the international language of business, travel, and air traffic control.
    e. Many countries have enacted laws to limit the use of English in their country.

32. Sikhism is a religion that arose from the confrontation between:
    a. Buddhism and Islam
    b. Islam and Hinduism
    c. Christianity and Islam
    d. Judaism and Hinduism
    e. Hinduism and Buddhism

33. Hinduism has not spread by expansion diffusion in modern times, but at one time it did spread by relocation diffusion as a result of:
    a. the transportation of Indian workers abroad during the colonial period
    b. conquest by militant groups from Sri Lanka
    c. forced relocation by due invaders from the North
    d. massive voluntary emigrations due to pull factors of Hinduism
    e. India's colonies in the East Africa realms

34. Nigeria is a multilingual country with many tribal boundaries where Christianity prevails in the south and ___________ in the north.
    a. Judaism
    b. Buddhism
    c. Sikhism
    d. Hinduism
    e. Islam

35. Using your mental maps and not thinking in terms of numbers of adherents of each religion, which of the following world religions is the LEAST widely diffused?
    a. Buddhism
    b. Christianity
    c. Islam
    d. Judaism
    e. Hinduism

36. Which of the following countries has not passed a national law based on protecting a language?
    a. Canada
    b. the United States
    c. Belgium
    d. France
    e. Romania

37. Which of the following is a reason for different countries in the same region having similar words for the word "milk"?
    a. language divergence
    b. language convergence
    c. language extinction
    d. language obstruction
    e. language commodification

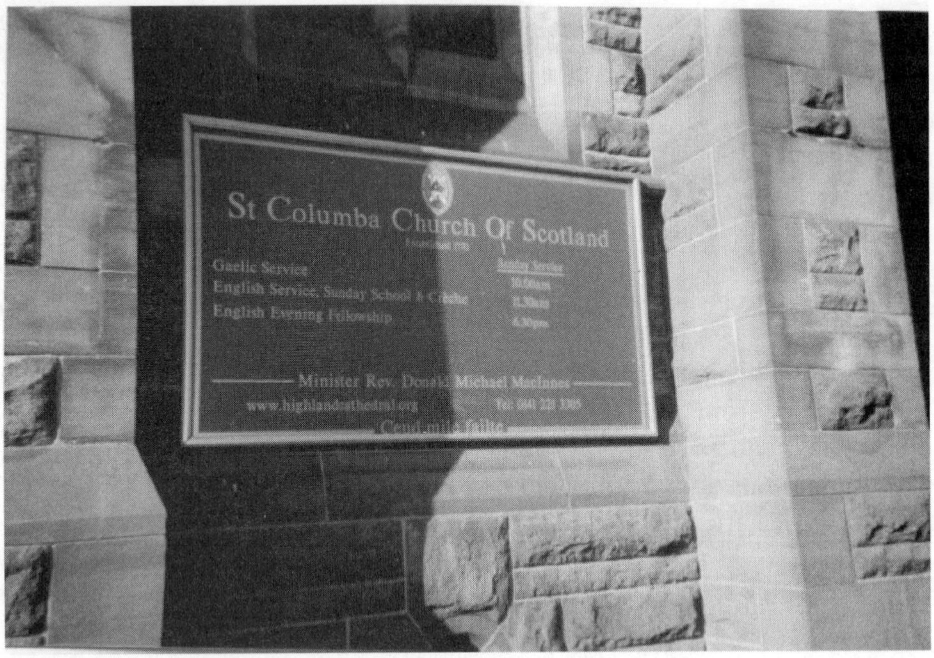

Source: © Paul T. Gray, Jr.

38. The sign above shows which geographic concept?
   a. linguistic revitalization
   b. religious syncretism
   c. language convergence
   d. universal religion
   e. lingua Franca

39. A federal state:
   a. has an unusually strong central government that controls the whole state equally
   b. is usually very large geographically and therefore may have very diverse peoples
   c. does not allow for the regional and cultural interests of minority groups
   d. is most likely to have very few, if any, substate units
   e. always has a capital city that is located in the middle of the country

40. Political states that have a religious government are known as:
   a. atheistic
   b. theocratic
   c. mercantile
   d. egalitarian
   e. nucleated

41. Which of the following is in the correct order regarding the establishment of boundaries?
   a. define – delimit – demarcate
   b. delimit – define – demarcate
   c. demarcate – delimit – define
   d. delimit – demarcate – define
   e. define – demarcate – delimit

42. In which of the following state morphologies is internal circulation/transportation/contact or other friction of distance issue *most* likely to be a major problem?
    a. fragmented
    b. compact
    c. perforated
    d. enclave
    e. prorupted

43. Which of the following phrases BEST defines "stateless nation"?
    a. many ethnic groups within several contiguous states with no one group dominating
    b. a group of people with a common culture and sense of unity but with no territory
    c. a single nation dispersed across and predominant in two or more states
    d. a distinct group of people occupying their own territory and sharing a common set of values
    e. an independent political entity that is not subdivided into regional or local units.

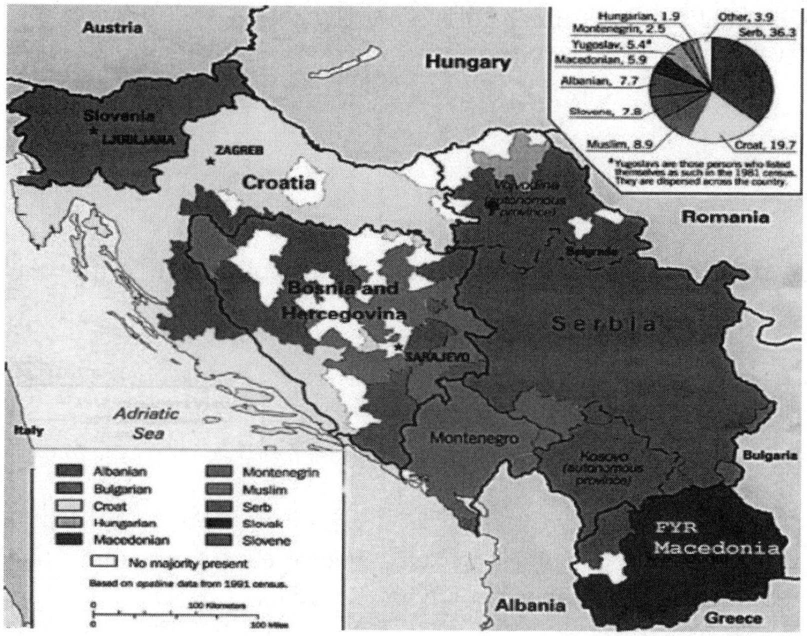

Source: © de Blij and Murphy, *Human Geography, Seventh Edition.* 2003, p. 217

44. Which of the following concepts does the map above best highlight?
    a. gerrymandering
    b. reapportionment
    c. shatterbelt
    d. neocolonialism
    e. annexation

45. The redistricting of congressional seats according to population after each census is known as:
    a. supranationalism
    b. gerrymandering
    c. majority-minority
    d. reapportionment
    e. federal

46. Which of the following is the BEST example of a set of stateless nations on the international stage?
    a. Basques – Palestinians – Kurds
    b. Cherokee –Sioux – Choctaw
    c. Lithuanians – Latvians – Estonians
    d. Thais – Vietnamese – Cambodians
    e. Bengalis – Burmese – Bhutanese

47. Organic theory postulates that the state's essential, lifegiving force is:
    a. population
    b. a strong military
    c. mobility
    d. territory
    e. power

48. Which of the following devolution groups/movements does not match with country/ countries?
    a. Catalonians – Spain
    b. Slovenians, Croatians, Bosnians – Yugoslavia
    c. Walloons/Flemish – Belgium
    d. Basques – Spain/France
    e. Sicilians –Greece

49. The effort by three or more countries that give up some measure of sovereignty to forge associations for common advantage and goals is known as:
    a. superinternationalism
    b. internationalism
    c. supranationalism
    d. intranationalism
    e. neocolonialism

50. The Peace of Westphalia is MOST important to the study of political geography because it:
    a. was the treaty that ended the Thirty Years' War
    b. finally helped the French make peace with Germany
    c. contained language that recognized the formation of states
    d. organized the first example of supranationalism
    e. diluted sovereignty and self-determination of states

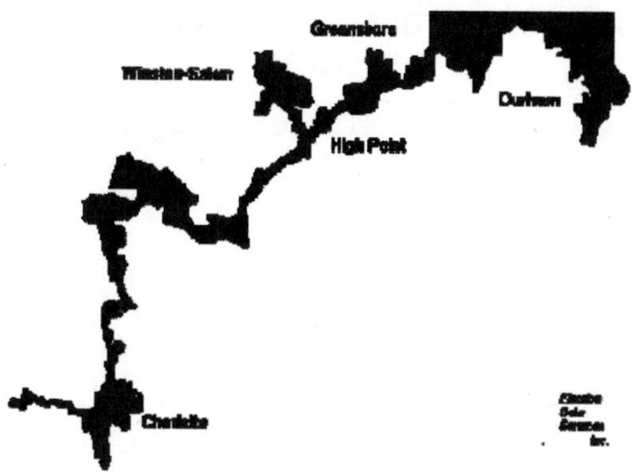

Source: Reproduced with permission from Election Data Services, Inc.

51. The map of a North Carolina congressional district above is indicative of:
    a. geometric boundaries
    b. supranationalism
    c. gerrymandering
    d. devolution
    e. core-peripheries

52. The motives for most examples of supranational cooperation, such as NAFTA and MERCOSUR, by the late 1990s were:
    a. mutual defense
    b. ethnic identification
    c. economic
    d. religious
    e. linguistic

Source: Murphy, A. B.; Jordan-Bychkov, Terry G.; and Jordan, Bella Bychdova. The European Culture Area: *A Systematic Geography, Fifth Edition* (Lanham, MD: Rowman & Littlefield, 2009), p. 168.

53. The spatial pattern of major roads meeting in the center of the map above likely indicates which kind of state?
    a. microstate
    b. fragmented state
    c. federal state
    d. perforated state
    e. unitary state

54. The extractive sector is also known as the _____________ sector, whereas the service sector is also known as the _____________ sector.
   a. secondary; quinary
   b. tertiary; secondary
   c. primary; tertiary
   d. quaternary; primary
   e. quinary; quaternary

55. Which of the following is CORRECT with regard to plant origins?
   a. Southeast Asia – watermelon, bamboo, beans
   b. Mesoamerica – maize (corn), squash, beans
   c. Southwest Asia – millets, water chestnuts, peanuts
   d. eastern India – tomatoes, potatoes, okra
   e. Ethiopia and East African Highlands – rice, bananas, bamboo

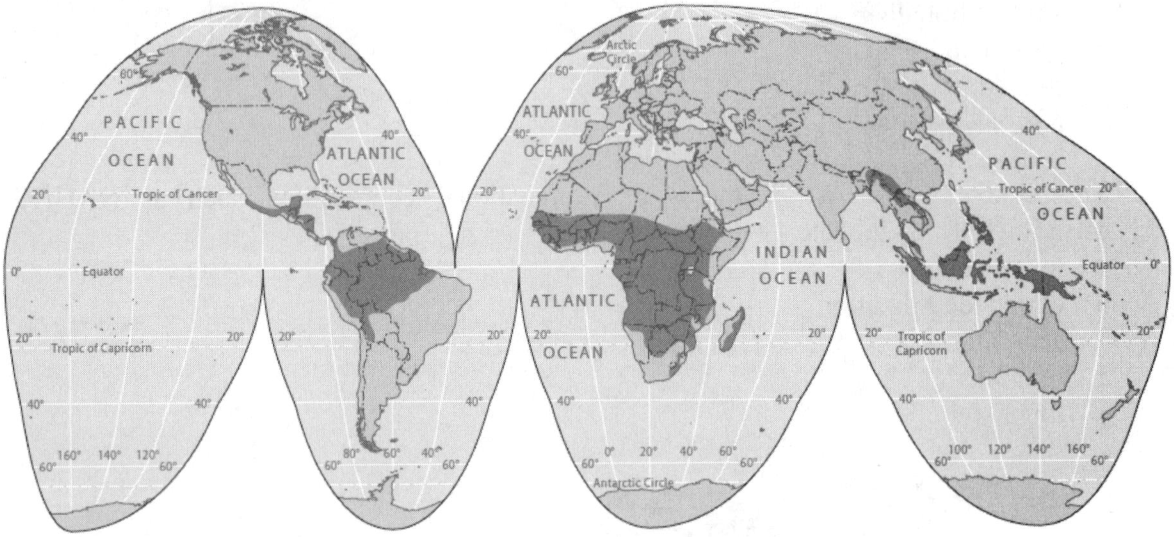

Source: © E. H. Fouberg, A. B. Murphy, H. J. de Blij, and John Wiley & Sons, Inc.

56. The shaded areas on the map above most likely depict which of the following types of agricultural practice?
   a. livestocking
   b. commercial
   c. hydroponics
   d. subsistence
   e. dairying

Use the following excerpt from the *New York Times* World section, January 25, 2008, issue to answer question 57.

"Instead of counting on free markets to generate opportunities spontaneously, the nonprofit groups managing some of the grants will intervene to help farmers form groups to sell goods in bulk and provide them with access to the agronomic advice, processing facilities and transportation they need to take advantage of growing markets for products like milk and coffee. In Kenya, Rwanda and Uganda, for example, Heifer International—working with other groups and institutions—will help women who tend cows gain access to refrigeration plants, enabling them to sell milk for distribution to stores distant from their farms."

57. Which of the following best exemplifies the agricultural issues in the quote above?
    a. Von Thünen's model has been made partially obsolete.
    b. Kenyan farmers are vertically integrating their practices.
    c. Extensive commercial agriculture is taking place in the developing world.
    d. A shift from traditional agriculture to agribusiness is becoming evident.
    e. Women in Kenya are becoming plantation farmers.

58. The growth and integration of the Roman Empire was greatly facilitated by a:
    a. road system
    b. lack of different languages
    c. conurbation effort
    d. lack of foreign enemies
    e. good postal system

59. Which of the following describes a city's position relative to much-traveled transport routes, production of farmland, and manufacturing and other towns/cities?
    a. site
    b. nucleation
    c. exurbanization
    d. situation
    e. rank-size

60. The urban hierarchy from the bottom up is best described by which of the following?
    a. village – hamlet – city – town – metropolis
    b. hamlet – town – city - metropolis – megalopolis
    c. town- village – hamlet – city – metropolis
    d. hamlet - city – town – village – megalopolis
    e. megalopolis – metropolis – city – town – hamlet

61. Which of the following is LEAST correct regarding professional sports and urban geography?
    a. Higher order functions such as professional sports teams are usually located at the top of the rank-size hierarchy.
    b. Smaller cities usually have professional sports teams because they have the most loyal and rabid fans.
    c. Professional sports teams have both increased since 1950 and diffused to the South and the West in the United States.
    d. The NHL has diffused to the southern and western states following the general shift in U.S. population.
    e. Having professional sports teams is a major characteristic of being an important city.

62. Which of the following is a CORRECT statement concerning the *spacing* of human settlements?
    a. Villages are separated by great distances.
    b. Large cities tend to be closer together than smaller ones.
    c. Towns are farther apart than cities.
    d. Large cities tend to be farther apart than smaller cities.
    e. A megalopolis tends to be geographically small.

63. The greatest number of workers in a city or town's economic base is in the __________ sector.
    a. agricultural
    b. basic
    c. quasi-basic
    d. manufacturing
    e. nonbasic

64. The rehabilitation of deteriorated inner city areas is also referred to as:
    a. commercialization
    b. suburbanization
    c. gesellschaft
    d. nucleation
    e. gentrification

Source: © Rob Crandall/ The Image Works.

65. This photo taken near a large metropolitan CBD most likely represents which of the following?
    a. megalopolis
    b. edge city
    c. village
    d. ethnic neighborhood
    e. tenement

66. Core countries are characterized by all of the following **EXCEPT:**
    a. high metals consumption
    b. low employment in agriculture
    c. high caloric diet
    d. low-protein intake
    e. high literacy rates

67. Which of the following is an example of a business/industry in the primary sector?
    a. a chewing gum factory
    b. an iron ore mine
    c. an insurance company
    d. a private university
    e. a call center

68. Which of the following theories/models/concepts declares that prosperity is sustained in the core, whereas poverty is sustained in the periphery
    a. organic
    b. modernization
    c. dependency
    d. secondary
    e. time–space convergence

69. Which of the factors of industrial location listed is INACCURATE?
    a. The periphery must sell raw materials to the core to procure foreign capital and currency.
    b. The core keeps prices of goods low by switching from supplier to supplier in the periphery.
    c. Low wages mean lower-priced goods and lead to flooded markets of cheaply priced goods.
    d. Highly developed industrial centers have highly developed transport systems.
    e. Transport costs tend to be a minimally important factor that a firm considers in location.

70. Which of the following transportation distance/cost to transportation mode associations is CORRECT?
    a. short – water
    b. intermediate – railroad
    c. long – truck
    d. intermediate – water
    e. short – air

71. According to Rostow's model, highly developed countries are in stages:
    a. 3 and 4
    b. 1 and 2
    c. 2, 3, and 4
    d. 5 and 1
    e. 4 and 5

72. Close proximity to the market is more significant in industrial locations when the commodity/finished product is:
    a. small and/or lightweight
    b. high in value
    c. bulky and/or heavy
    d. low in value
    e. small and/or expensive

73. Among the significant recent innovations in bulk transport is the development of:
    a. container systems
    b. pipeline systems
    c. better railroad lines
    d. more efficient trucks
    e. air freight

74. Weber did for industry what von Thünen did for agriculture by predicting ways to minimize costs. What were the three basic costs Weber focused on minimizing?
    a. labor – deglomeration – other factors
    b. transportation – labor – excise taxes
    c. agglomeration – transportation – labor
    d. labor – food costs – transportation
    e. raw materials – agglomeration – owner preference

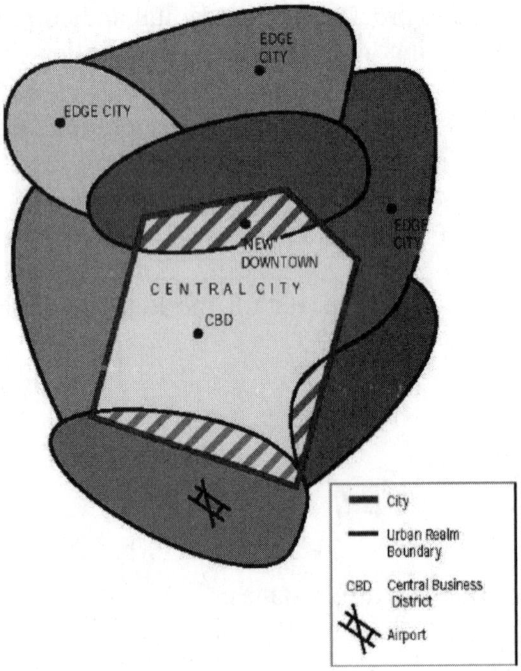

From de Blij, Murphy, and Fouberg, *Human Geography, Eighth Edition,* 2007, p. 279. Adapted with permission from: T. Hartshorn and P. O. Muller, "Suburban Downtowns and the Transformation of Metropolitan Atlanta's Business Landscape," *Urban Landscape* 10 (1989), p. 375.

75. Which of the urban models is shown above?
    a. central place theory
    b. urban realms model
    c. sector model
    d. multiple nuclei model
    e. concentric zone model

FREE-RESPONSE QUESTIONS

Directions: You have 75 minutes to answer all three of the following questions. It is recommended that you spend approximately one-third of your time (25 minutes) on each question. It is suggested that you take up to 5 minutes of this time to plan and outline each answer. Although a formal essay is not required, it is not enough to answer a question by merely listing facts. Illustrate your answers with substantive geographic examples where appropriate. Be sure that you number each of your answers, including individual parts, in the answer booklet as the questions are numbered below.

Answer all items using the A, B, C, etc., format

1. Use the maps to answer the following questions:
   A. What geographic concept is being shown or demonstrated in the ***set of three maps*** (on this and the next page) of Russellville, Arkansas?
   B. Using the concept you named in Part A, identify the map that shows the least amount of distance and explain why this is so.
   C. Explain which map would be most useful in planning a trip from Russellville to Clarksville and which map would be most useful in navigating to Old Post Road Park.

1

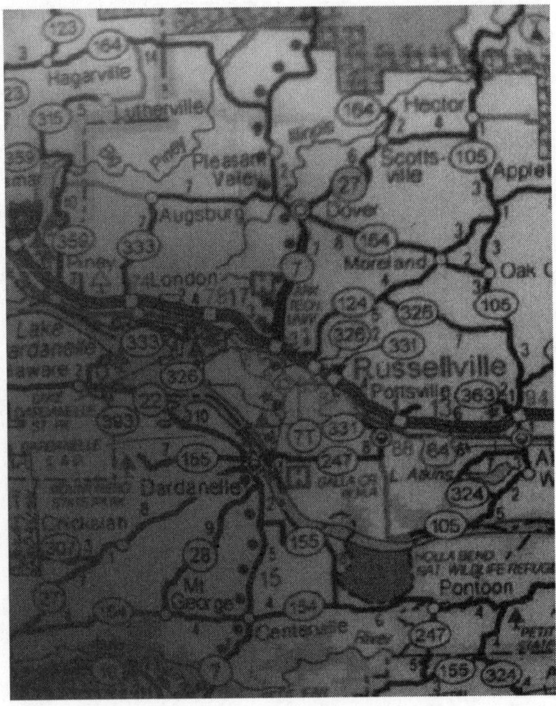

2

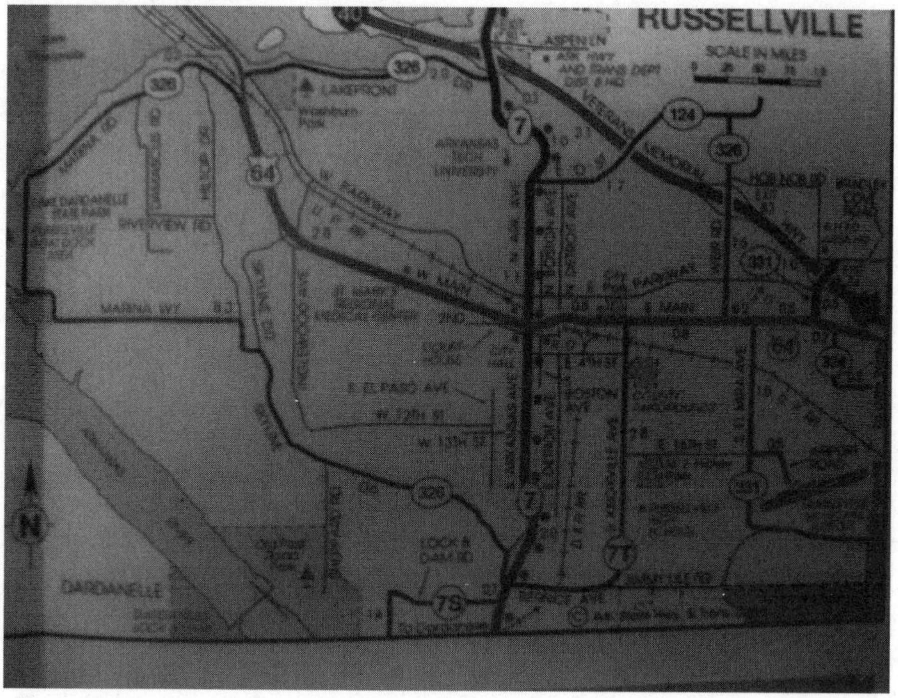

3

Photos of map used by permission of the Arkansas State Highway and Transportation Department, Little Rock, Arkansas. Map published in 2011.

2. Geographers use regions to help define and delimit the similarities and differences in places.
   A. Define formal, functional, and perceptual regions.
   B. Give one real-world example of each type of region.
   C. Identify the type of region that is most difficult to define.
   D. Give two reasons to explain why this type of region (Part C answer) is more difficult to define. Give specific details in your answer.

3. Agriculture has been vital for human population growth and expansion.
   A. Explain the geography behind the origin of agriculture and explain why it occurred in those locations.
   B. Explain what the Columbian Exchange was.
   C. Take one region of the world and explain how it was impacted by the Columbian Exchange.

SECTION 4: AP HUMAN GEOGRAPHY
EXAM TWO

You should allow 60 minutes to choose the BEST answer for each of the following items.

1. The location of a place using the latitude-longitude grid is called:
   a. relative location
   b. absolute location
   c. central location
   d. referenced location
   e. actual location

2. The set of processes that are increasing and deepening interactions, interdependence, and relationships is known as:
   a. possibilism
   b. spatial interaction
   c. globalization
   d. geocaching
   e. environmental determinism

3. The areas where civilizations developed and innovated are called:
   a. culture systems
   b. primary regions
   c. culture hearths
   d. clustered regions
   e. indigenous area

4. The diagram below shows an area of interactions and connections that are best represented by which region?
   a. perceptual
   b. formal
   c. vernacular
   d. cognitive
   e. functional

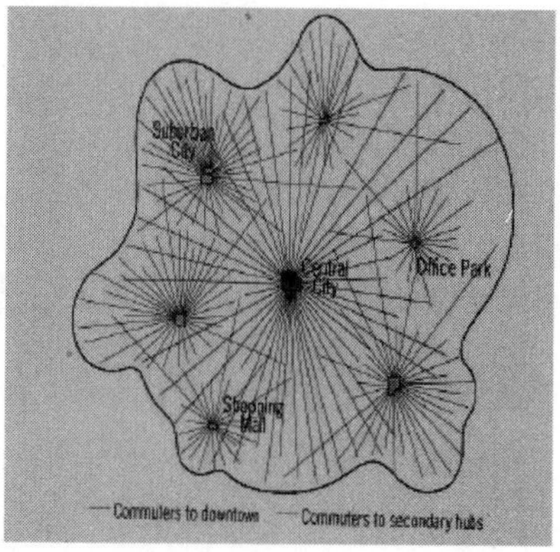

From de Blij and Murphy, *Human Geography, Seventh Edition,* 2003, p. 17.

5. The process of spreading an idea from its source area to other areas or cultures is known as:
   a. possibilism
   b. simulation
   c. adaptation
   d. sharing
   e. diffusion

6. The technique whereby geographers use satellites and aircraft to monitor, among other things, environmental changes on the Earth's surface is known as:
   a. remote sensing
   b. terra incognita
   c. cultural ecology
   d. sequent occupance
   e. perceptual region

7. An outsider traveling into the southern part of the United States might begin to hear slower speech patterns and country/gospel music on the radio, encounter increasing numbers of Baptist churches, read grits on restaurant menus, and see large front porches on houses. The traveler's thoughts about these characteristics might form the basis of his or her notions of which type of region?
   a. perceptual region
   b. formal region
   c. stimulus region
   d. transculturation region
   e. culture hearth

8. Which of the following statements is FALSE concerning the world's population?
   a. Artificial birth control use is higher in core countries.
   b. Population growth rates differ from place to place.
   c. Uneducated women usually have higher fertility rates.
   d. High fertility rates tend to be in overpopulated areas.
   e. Population is evenly distributed over the Earth's surface.

9. The *arithmetic* population density for a country is determined by dividing the total:
   a. number of city dwellers by rural people
   b. area of square miles by five
   c. minority population of the area
   d. population by the total land area
   e. population by the number of farmers

10. An age-sex diagram, such as the pyramid on the right, with a large base, steep sides. and a very pointed top most likely indicates a:
   a. slow-growth country
   b. gay/lesbian neighborhood
   c. migrant worker community
   d. rapid growth country
   e. city with a prison

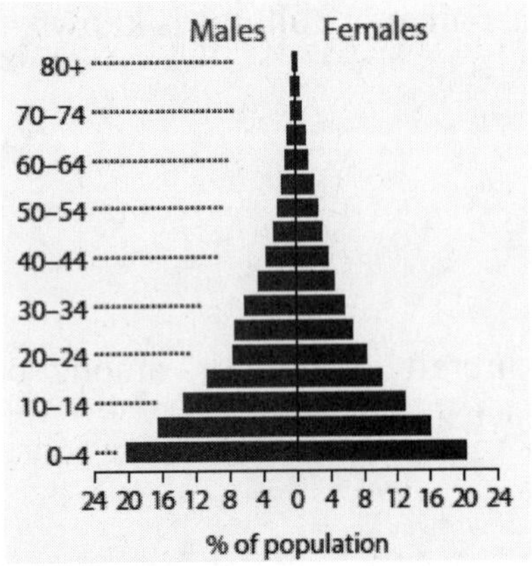

Source: Fouberg, Murphy, and de Blij. *Human Geography, Tenth Edition,* p. 61.

11. In examining a population density map of East Asia, a pattern of decreasing population one would see on the map would be from:
   a. south to north
   b. north to south
   c. the interior toward the coast
   d. the coast toward the interior
   e. the northern coast to the southern coast

12. Migration streams into the United States:
    a. were at their lowest point between World War I and World War II.
    b. have increased through every twenty-year period since 1840.
    c. came to an apex between 1840 and 1860 as eastern Europeans arrived.
    d. saw large declines in the 1990s due to Clinton administration policies.
    e. were increased in 1880–1900 as large numbers of Hispanics began to enter.

Use the images below to answer question 13.

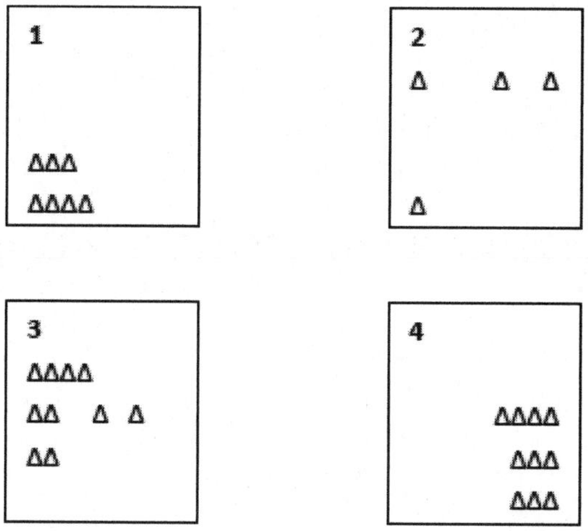

13. Using your knowledge of population density and distribution, which two of the four boxes have the highest distribution of triangles?
    a. 1, 2
    b. 3, 4
    c. 4, 1
    d. 2, 3
    e. 2, 4

14. If a population increases by a uniform amount during a series of equal time periods, the increase is said to be:
    a. linear
    b. compounded
    c. exponential
    d. modest
    e. doubling

15. Using your knowledge of natural increase, if a population is growing at an average rate of 2 percent, its doubling time would be approximately ____ years.
    a. 20
    b. 25
    c. 50
    d. 35
    e. 10

16. In 1798, Thomas Malthus published an essay in which he claimed that population increased at a(n) ____________ rate, while the means of subsistence grew at a(n) ____________ rate.
   a. linear; exponential
   b. cultural; ethnic
   c. arithmetic; geometric
   d. declining; increasing
   e. exponential; linear

17. In which stage of the demographic transition would the age-sex diagram to the right most likely be located?
   a. 1
   b. 2
   c. 3
   d. 4
   e. 1 or 4

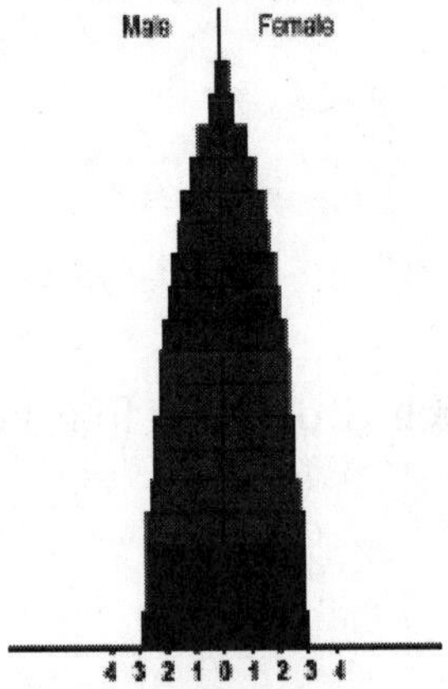

18. The problem with using *arithmetic* population density to investigate the population pattern of a country is that such a density figure does not take into consideration:
   a. annual population increases
   b. internal clustering patterns
   c. annexation of new territory
   d. possible loss of territory
   e. external political forces

19. The long-term relocation of an individual, household, or group to a new location outside the community of origin is called:
   a. resettlement
   b. transportation
   c. migration
   d. transmovement
   e. transhumance

20. An age-sex diagram with high numbers of people in the upper age cohorts is most indicative of a:
   a. city with a large college-aged population
   b. town devastated by a major tornado
   c. country with high rates of dowry deaths
   d. country with very low fertility rates
   e. city with a large retirement community

21. In the United States during the 1980s and 1990s, internal migration streams were:
   a. moving generally from west to east and south to north
   b. moving generally from west to east and north to south
   c. completely static
   d. moving generally from east to west and south to north
   e. moving generally from east to west and north to south

22. In which former European country did a dreadful conflict push as many as three million people to migrate from their homes in the 1990s?
   a. Poland
   b. Germany
   c. France
   d. Ukraine
   e. Yugoslavia

23. The measure of the number of children born to women of childbearing age in the population is called the:
   a. actual birth rate
   b. crude birth rate
   c. natural increase rate
   d. adjusted birth rate
   e. total fertility rate

24. Which of the following countries would be predicted to have the highest CDR?
   a. Ukraine
   b. Japan
   c. Indonesia
   d. Sierra Leone
   e. Portugal

25. Ravenstein's gravity model of migration stated all of the following EXCEPT:
   a. Net migration is only a fraction of gross migration between two places.
   b. The majority of migrants move only a short distance.
   c. Rural residents are far less likely to migrate than their urban counterparts.
   d. Families are less likely to make international moves than young adults.
   e. Migrants who move longer distances tend to choose big-city destinations.

26. The most widely used and diffused Indo-European language in the world today is:
    a. English
    b. German
    c. Spanish
    d. French
    e. Basque

27. Which of these best describes the world's religions from largest to smallest?
    a. Christianity – Hinduism – Islam – Sikhism – Judaism
    b. Islam – Christianity – Hinduism – Judaism – Chinese religions
    c. Buddhism – Christianity – Islam – Hinduism – Sikhism
    d. Christianity – Islam – Hinduism – Buddhism – Sikhism
    e. Christianity – Buddhism – Hinduism – Judaism – Islam

28. To which subfamily of languages does English belong?
    a. Romance
    b. Germanic
    c. Slavic
    d. Celtic
    e. Druid

29. The presence of fast-food restaurants tends to make a cultural landscape more:
    a. heterogeneous
    b. religious
    c. rural
    d. homogeneous
    e. isolated

30. Wilbur Zelinsky attempted to define cultural landscapes and perceptual regions by using information found in which of the following?
    a. signs
    b. ethnicities
    c. cameras
    d. journals
    e. phonebooks

31. The island in the Mediterranean Sea that had to be partitioned because two cultures, the Greeks and Turks, could not get along is:
    a. Malta
    b. Sicily
    c. Corsica
    d. Sardinia
    e. Cyprus

32. The world's most populated Islamic state is:
    a. Iran
    b. Pakistan
    c. Indonesia
    d. the Philippines
    e. Saudi Arabia

33. Which country would most accurately satisfy the definition of a nation-state?
    a. Kurdistan
    b. United States
    c. Japan
    d. Mexico
    e. South Africa

34. The element most essential and common to the world's political states is:
    a. ethnicity
    b. capital
    c. territory
    d. religion
    e. coastline

35. Which of the following phrases BEST defines "stateless nation"?
    a. many ethnic groups within several contiguous states with no one group dominating
    b. a group of people with a common culture and sense of unity but with no territory
    c. a single nation dispersed across and predominant in two or more states
    d. a distinct group of people of shared history who occupy their own territory
    e. an independent political entity that is not subdivided into regional or local units

36. Many of Europe's unitary states, and their administrative frameworks were designed to:
    a. ensure the central government's authority over all parts of the state
    b. allow maximum local autonomy for the citizens of the country
    c. control the core area and let the hinterlands have autonomy
    d. create conditions for a transition to a federal state government
    e. expand the rights of nonmajority tribal and linguistic groups

37. Which academic field of inquiry deals with the spatial aspects of voting systems, voting behavior, and voter representation?
    a. government geography
    b. electoral geography
    c. congressional geography
    d. apportionment geography
    e. district geography

38. Which of the following is NOT an example of devolution or devolutionary pressure in Europe?
    a. the breakup of Yugoslavia
    b. the "velvet revolution" in Czechoslovakia
    c. local autonomy in Wales from the UK
    d. the Basque separatist movement in Spain
    e. reunification of East and West Germany

39. At the Conference of Berlin, the European colonial powers delimited the boundaries of:
    a. Asia
    b. South America
    c. Central America
    d. Africa
    e. Antarctica

40. Geographer K. W. Robinson once said that this type of state is "the most expressive of all types of government" and "does not create unity out of diversity; rather, it enables the two to coexist." To which type of state was Robinson referring?
    a. unitary
    b. multicore
    c. primate
    d. federal
    e. tribal

41. MERCOSUR is a supranational organization located in:
    a. Australia
    b. Africa
    c. Europe
    d. Asia
    e. South America

42. Delimited boundaries are best described generally as:
    a. having been officially drawn on a map
    b. being evident by fences, stones, markers, and so on
    c. having been simply described through treaties
    d. being drawn predominantly in geometric lines
    e. following landscape features such as rivers

43. The Green Revolution was responsible for all of the following EXCEPT:
    a. increased world cereal grains production
    b. decreased the overall number of farmers
    c. decreased the number of jobs available for women
    d. was instrumental in famine relief
    e. increased arable land by over 75 percent

44. Which type of agriculture is generally located on the west coasts of continents; includes the dry, summer climates of southern California, central Chile, South Africa's cape, Greece, and other areas; and grows crops such as grapes and citrus?
    a. chapparal
    b. Mediterranean
    c. commercial
    d. plantation
    e. luxury

45. Which of these products experienced an increase in demand in the 1970s owing to more health benefits and the rise of fast-food restaurants?
    a. chicken
    b. duck
    c. mutton
    d. pork
    e. dairy

46. Plantation agriculture is characterized by all of the following EXCEPT:
    a. primarily grow only one crop
    b. crops grown largely for export
    c. subsistence crops farmed by local people
    d. located on the best land in the area
    e. owned by multinational corporations

47. Poultry production in the United States:
    a. is spatially oriented to the more rural regions of the country
    b. decreased with the emergence of conglomerates like Tyson
    c. is naturally in urban areas as von Thünen's model predicts
    d. dropped because of lower nutritional values in chicken meat
    e. has been outsourced to countries such as Chile

48. Which of the following agricultural operations is characterized by sizable capital, low labor input per unit of land, large land units, and medium/long distance from market?
    a. intensive subsistence farming
    b. shifting cultivation
    c. commercial wheat farming
    d. patch agriculture
    e. hunting/gathering

49. Which Asian country owes its vast cotton fields/production to the influence of colonial Britain?
    a. Pakistan
    b. Sri Lanka
    c. the Philippines
    d. India
    e. Bangladesh

50. Which of the following is NOT an example of shifting agriculture?
    a. metes and bounds
    b. slash and burn
    c. swidden
    d. milpa
    e. patch

51. According to von Thünen's model and principles, which of the following would be predicted to be the farthest from the market?
    a. strawberries
    b. cattle
    c. tomatoes
    d. corn
    e. forest belt

52. Which of the following statements about organic agriculture is FALSE?
    a. The markets for these products are largely located in core countries.
    b. Market prices are low since the costs of organic agriculture remain low.
    c. Organic agriculture reduces the amount of chemicals put into the soil and water.
    d. Some countries are approaching 10 percent sales figures of organic agriculture.
    e. Taste and health benefits are two reasons many demand organic products.

53. The system of measuring land which usually had a starting point from rivers, canals and roads was the system.
    a. long lot
    b. feudal
    c. township-and-range
    d. village
    e. metes-and-bounds

54. Each of the following statements about suburbanization is correct EXCEPT:
    a. The high number of World War II soldier casualties limited the demand for housing for a decade.
    b. The completion of the interstate highway system made commuting to the workplace easier.
    c. Industry was attracted to the suburbs by modern plant facilities and plenty of parking spaces for employees.
    d. Service industries developed as a result of the purchasing power and the available suburban labor force.
    e. As people moved to the suburbs, regional shopping centers replaced the CBD retail districts.

55. The population growth center in the United States from 1790 to the present has generally moved:
    a. north and south
    b. west and east
    c. north and east
    d. east and west
    e. south and west

56. The poor living conditions of European manufacturing cities were eventually improved by government intervention, legislation, recognition of workers' rights, and the introduction of:
    a. city planning and zoning
    b. more efficient factories
    c. a substitute for coal
    d. suburbanization
    e. blockbusting

57. According to the text, the earliest civilization occurred in:
    a. Andean America
    b. Indus Valley
    c. Mediterranean Europe
    d. Mesopotamia
    e. Nile Valley

58. A town is defined as a place where an assemblage of goods/services is available with a:
    a. good highway system
    b. minimum of 25,000 people
    c. public transportation system
    d. hinterland
    e. recognizable suburban area

59. The dominant city of the North American interior is:
    a. Kansas City
    b. St. Louis
    c. Cleveland
    d. Denver
    e. Chicago

60. The spatial process of clustering by commercial enterprises for mutual advantage and benefit is called:
    a. relocation
    b. diffusion
    c. gravitation
    d. agglomeration
    e. blockbusting

61. Harris and Ullman's multiple nuclei model of urban structure arose from the idea that _________ was losing its dominant position in the metropolitan city to other competition.
   a. the exurb
   b. the edge city
   c. public transportation
   d. the suburb
   e. the CBD

62. The Latin American city structure model to the right has all of the following elements **EXCEPT:**
   a. squatter areas located on the outer ring of the city
   b. very poor people living close to the very wealthy
   c. a mall area characterized by open pedestrian zones
   d. distinct upper-income suburbs located on the periphery
   e. gangs and drug lords located in the Perifico

A NEW AND IMPROVED MODEL OF LATIN AMERICAN CITY STRUCTURE

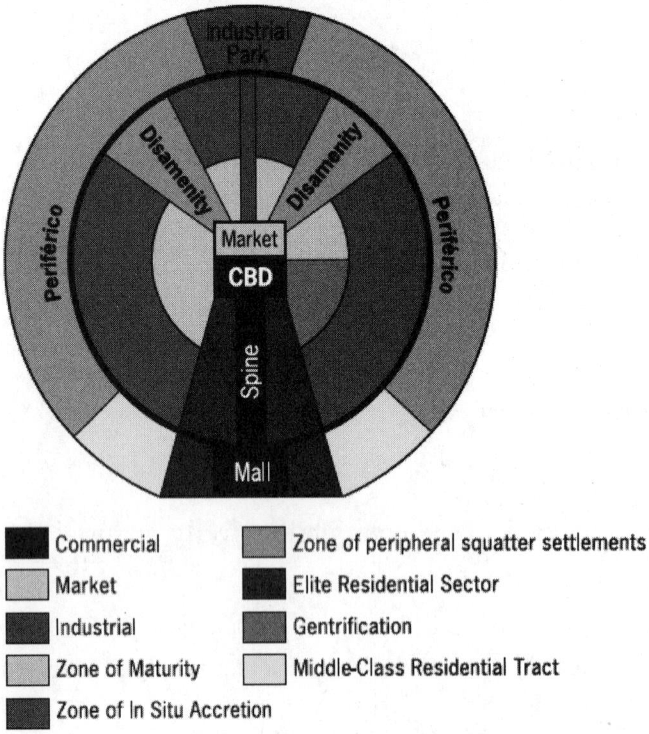

From Fouberg, Murphy, and de Blij, *Human Geography,* p. 279. Adapted with permission from L. Ford, "A New and Improved Model of Latin American City Structure," *The Geographical Review* 86 (1996), p. 438.

63. The sector model of urban structure by Homer Hoyt promoted what important aspects of urban structure and life?
    a. neighborhood ethnicity/socioeconomics
    b. bid rent/transport routes
    c. gender studies/gay-lesbian neighborhoods
    d. public housing/poor people
    e. irrelevance of the CBD/edge cities

64. The ________________ model illustrates the theoretical idea that two vendors selling ice cream on a beach would eventually be selling back-to-back to maximize the number of customers and profits.
    a. Burgess
    b. Weber
    c. Hotelling
    d. Losch
    e. Hoyt

65. Which of the following is NOT a characteristic of a "periphery country" in the capitalist economic system?
    a. narrower range of consumer products than in core countries
    b. exporting high-quality finished goods
    c. less advanced technology
    d. lower wages than core countries
    e. exporting raw materials to core countries

66. Which of the terms listed below describes the entrenchment of the old system of dominance by core countries on periphery countries under an *economic* rather than direct political/military control?
    a. colonialism
    b. developing dominance
    c. neo-colonialism
    d. transhumance
    e. neo-nihilism

67. The theory that states prosperity is sustained in the core while poverty is sustained in the periphery is known as:
    a. organic
    b. modernization
    c. dependency
    d. secondary
    e. time–space convergence

68. The principal structuralist alternative to Rostow's model of economic development is known as:
    a. the "takeoff" model
    b. the liberal model
    c. the modernization model
    d. dependency theory
    e. least-cost theory

69. Extractive activities are a synonym for which of the following?
    a. primary
    b. secondary
    c. tertiary
    d. quaternary
    e. quinary

70. The economic boom on East Asia's Pacific Rim is based substantially on the low-cost of which of the following?
    a. raw materials
    b. transportation
    c. labor
    d. power
    e. food

71. Outsourcing of call center services to India is done for all of the following **EXCEPT:**
    a. stable democracy
    b. English speakers
    c. transport costs
    d. college graduates
    e. labor costs

72. For most goods, the cheapest method of transport over short distances is by:
    a. railroad
    b. truck
    c. ships
    d. pipeline
    e. air

73. In northern Mexico's border region with the United States, there is a manufacturing zone where plants, mainly owned by U.S. companies, transform imported, duty-free components or raw materials into finished industrial products. These plants are called:
    a. maquiladoras
    b. braceros
    c. pulques
    d. favelas
    e. bulk-reducers

74. According to the text, which of the following city sets contains the three most dominant world cities?
    a. London - Tokyo - Beijing
    b. New York – London - Tokyo
    c. Shanghai - Paris - New York
    d. Tokyo - London-Paris
    e. Los Angeles - New York - Chicago

75. A location along a transport route where goods must be transferred from one mode to another is known as a(n):
    a. maquiladora
    b. agglomeration
    c. technopole
    d. break-of-bulk
    e. buffer zone

FREE RESPONSE QUESTIONS FOR EXAM TWO

1. One of the important models in human geography is von Thünen's model. Answer the following questions about products and agricultural markets.
   A. Define market gardening and identify where it fits into von Thünen's model.
   B. Give three examples of market garden products.
   C. For two of the items named in B, explain two reasons why it would be produced at that location (this means two different items with different reasons).

2. Languages and language issues are a major topic of study in cultural geography. Answer the following items about languages.
   A. Define lingua franca, pidgin, and Creole
   B. For each term in item A, at what geographic scale would each usually occur (large, medium, or small)?
   C. Using the tables and your knowledge of population, diffusion, language, or other factors, choose two (2) languages that changed between the tables. For each language you chose, give two (2) geographic explanations for the changes between Tables 1, 2, and/or 3.

World Language Rankings—Global Number of Speakers

Table 1

1994–1995

1. Mandarin	**4. Hindi**
2. English	**5. Russian**
3. Spanish	**6. Bengali**

Source: de Blij and Murphy, Human Geography, 6th ed.

Table 2

2002–2003

1. Mandarin	**4. Spanish**
2. English	**5. Arabic**
3. Hindi	**6. Bengali**

Source: de Blij and Murphy, Human Geography, 7th ed.

Table 3

2011

1. Mandarin	**6. Bengali**
2. Spanish	**6. Portuguese**
2. English	**8. Russian**
4. Arabic	**9. Japanese**
5. Hindi	**10. German**

Source: http://geography.about.com/od/culturalgeography/a/10languages.htm

3. Today's world is a fast-paced and ever-changing mix of globalizing technology. These create situations that require a balance between the global and the local scales.
   A. Describe one specific technology from the twentieth/twenty-first centuries and explain how it has helped make the world a more connected place.
   B. Describe one specific technology from the twentieth/twenty-first centuries and explain how it has helped maintain local cultures.

Notes

Notes

Notes

Notes

Notes